Rebels

REBELS is an exciting and innovative new series looking at rebel groups and their place in global politics. Written by experts, the books serve as definitive introductions to the individual organizations, whilst seeking to place them within a broader geographical and political framework. They examine the origins, ideology and future direction of each group, whilst posing such questions as: When does a 'rebel' political movement become a 'terrorist' organization? and What are the social and economic drivers behind political violence?

Provocative and original, the series is essential reading for anyone interested in how rebel groups operate today.

FORTHCOMING

Garry Leech, *The FARC*

Zapatistas

Rebellion from the Grassroots to the Global

ALEX KHASNABISH

Fernwood Publishing
HALIFAX & WINNIPEG

Zed Books
LONDON & NEW YORK

Zapatistas: Rebellion from the Grassroots to the Global
was first published in 2010.

Published in Canada by Fernwood Publishing Ltd,
32 Oceanvista Lane, Black Point, Nova Scotia BOJ 1BO
www.fernwoodpublishing.ca

Published in the rest of the world by
Zed Books Ltd, 7 Cynthia Street, London N1 9JF, UK
and Room 400, 175 Fifth Avenue, New York, NY 10010, USA
www.zedbooks.co.uk

Designed and typeset in Monotype Bulmer by illuminati,
Grosmont, www.illuminatibooks.co.uk
Index by John Barker
Cover designed by www.alice-marwick.co.uk
Printed and bound in Great Britain by CPI Antony Rowe

Distributed in the USA exclusively by Palgrave Macmillan, a division of
St Martin's Press, LLC, 175 Fifth Avenue, New York, NY 10010, USA

A catalogue record for this book is available from the British Library

Library of Congress Cataloging in Publication Data available

Library and Archives Canada Cataloguing in Publication

Khasnabish, Alex, 1976–
   Zapatistas : rebellion from the grassroots
to the global / Alex Khasnabish.
Co-published by: Zed Books.
Includes bibliographical references.
ISBN 978-1-55266-357-8
   1. Ejército Zapatista de Liberación Nacional (Mexico)—History.
2. Chiapas (Mexico)—History—Peasant Uprising, 1994-.   3. Indians of
Mexico—Mexico—Chiapas—Social conditions—20th century.   4. Social
movements—Mexico—Chiapas—History—20th century. I. Title.
F1256.K53 2009   972´.750836
C2009-907086-3

   ISBN   978 1 84813 207 8 hb   (Zed Books)
   ISBN   978 1 84813 208 5 pb   (Zed Books)
   ISBN   978 1 84813 209 2 eb   (Zed Books)
   ISBN   978 1 55266 357 8 pb   (Fernwood Publishing)

Contents

Acknowledgements

WRITING only *seems* like a solitary activity. In reality, it is the product of a tremendous diversity of experiences, encounters, inspirations and influences. I'd like to take a moment to thank all of those — both individuals and collectives — who helped make this book. First, I need to express my deepest gratitude to and respect for the Zapatistas. My own political and intellectual development would have occurred very differently in the absence of this inspirational movement 'for humanity and against neoliberalism'. I hope this book does justice to the profound significance of the Zapatistas' dignified rebellion in defence of a world capable of holding many worlds.

Over the past decade, I have had the privilege of working with activists across Mexico, Canada and the United States whose political work has paid homage to the inspiration of Zapatismo. To those individuals and collectives — and particularly to those, from Peoples' Global Action and Big Noise Tactical, whose voices are included in this book — I offer my deepest thanks for sharing your thoughts, commitments and experiences with me. I hope this book contributes in some small way to our struggles for democracy, liberty, peace and justice.

I'd like to extend sincere thanks to Ken Barlow, commissioning editor at Zed Books, whose patience and richly constructive comments were essential to bringing this project to fruition. Thanks also go to Ellen Hallsworth, former commissioning editor at Zed Books, who worked enthusiastically with me in the formative stages of this book. I would also like to thank the production and publicity staff at Zed Books, as well as my anonymous reviewer, for their work on this book.

This book is dedicated to Candida Hadley and Indra Hadley-Khasnabish. To my partner Candida — to whom I owe a great debt for providing research and critical insight into the gendered politics of Zapatismo — our relationship is a constant reminder that building a better world is not a grand project imposed from above; it is something that rises up from below and is given shape and meaning in our social relationships with one another. Indra — your joyfulness, curiosity, love, sensitivity, imagination and intelligence give the lie to those who see in humanity only a will to competition, domination and power. This book is for you, and for rebels everywhere.

'Enough!'

INTRODUCTION

1 JANUARY 1994 was a day of many firsts: the first day, of course, of the new year; the first day of the North American Free Trade Agreement binding Canada, Mexico and the United States together in what would become the template for neoliberal capitalist trade arrangements; and the first day of the 'war against oblivion' declared by the Ejército Zapatista de Liberación Nacional (EZLN, the Zapatista Army of National Liberation). Rising up in arms from the jungles and canyons of the south-eastern Mexican state of Chiapas to seize towns and ranches and even to occupy the old colonial capital of Chiapas, San Cristóbal de las Casas, the EZLN declared their rebellion against the Mexican federal government, the Mexican federal army, and, most importantly, against a trajectory of racism, neglect, genocide and exploitation that began with the conquest of the Americas more than five hundred years ago. Declaring their intention to march on Mexico City, defeat the federal army and depose the corrupt government of Carlos Salinas, in order to allow for Mexicans to exercise free and democratic control over their lives and the life of their nation,

the Zapatistas made sure that after 1 January 1994 nothing would be the same again.

Responding to the shocking and politically humiliating insurgency, the Mexican government responded not only with brutal military force but by contending that

> A delicate situation has presented itself in just four of the 110 municipalities of Chiapas; in the remaining 106 conditions are normal. The violent groups present a mixture of interests, both national and foreign, and show affinities with other violent Central American factions. Some indigenous peoples have been recruited and without doubt manipulated. (Muñoz Ramírez 2008: 108–9)

Despite the Mexican government's attempts to spin the rebellion, in surprising and dramatic fashion people within Mexico and around the world with no pre-existing knowledge of or contact with the rebels responded to the Zapatistas not with fear but with hope. In the days that followed the uprising, several things became abundantly clear. First, the Zapatista rebels were mainly poor indigenous Mayans from Chiapas, not foreign insurgents; second, their demands were just and they spoke to the struggles of Mexicans and others around the world; third, Mexican civil society would not allow the army to massacre the Zapatistas, but neither would ordinary people support the path of armed struggle as a way to lasting social change. By 12 January 1994, as massive demonstrations within and outside of Mexico compelled President Carlos Salinas to declare a unilateral ceasefire and invite the EZLN to negotiations, the Zapatistas had been adopted by Mexican and international civil society as *rebels*, with all the allure, legitimacy and righteousness the term implies.

Rebel dignity

This book critically considers what has made the Zapatistas rebels in the eyes of so many within Mexico and around the world, rather than the 'professionals of violence' the Mexican government tried so very hard to cast them as. Beyond the imagery and allure of rebellion, this book also takes up the question of the significance and influence of the Zapatistas *as rebels* on regional, national and transnational terrains since their uprising began on New Year's Day 1994. Indeed, it is no exaggeration to say that in the absence of the Zapatista rebellion, the political landscape not only of Mexico but of the world would look dramatically different today. The questions that arise in relation to this are how, why and with what consequences? The answers lie within the Zapatista movement itself, as well as within the social and political context — both nationally and globally — within which it is situated. This book is an attempt to illuminate critically the rebel significance of the Zapatistas.

In most places, particularly in a post-9/11 context, initiating an armed rebellion against the internationally recognized government of a state would be reason enough to be labelled a threat to peace, security and sovereignty. Grievances aside, few groups are able to pose a fundamental — much less armed and insurrectionary — challenge to the dominant political power structure and avoid labels of criminality both domestically and internationally. The so-called 'War on Terror' — a temporally and spatially unlimited police action declared by the government of the United States and now taken up by a host of other states in the aftermath of the 9/11 terrorist attacks — has only served to expand the latitude dominant power structures have to apply a diverse array of repressive techniques to their challengers. On top of all of this, threats to territorial integrity and state sovereignty marshalled by dissident groups are among the most serious crimes within the framework of the international system of nation-states. So, in the face of all of this, how does an insurgent armed force declare war on the federal executive, the federal army, while announcing its intention to participate in building a new political system to replace the existing one and *not* be subject to charges of criminality and terrorism and the punitive measures they carry with them? In order to understand this and what it means in terms of the political significance of the Zapatistas nationally and transnationally it is necessary to understand the innovative, creative and dynamic form of radical struggle the Zapatistas have advanced not only since their 1994 uprising but since the birth of the EZLN a decade earlier.

In an attempt to explain the tremendous appeal of the Zapatistas nationally and internationally, many observers have commented on their limited and deliberate use of violence. While the EZLN emerged in 1994 and continues to this day as an armed insurrectionary force, from the outset of the rebellion its use of violence bore marked differences to that of other insurrectionary movements in Latin America and around the world. It is certainly true that the Zapatistas have always been very careful to avoid the indiscriminate use of force and the targeting of civilians. From the beginning of their uprising they also explicitly committed themselves to the Geneva Convention, demanded to be recognized as a belligerent force, declared war rather than engaging in acts of terror or destabilization, and called for international actors like the Red Cross to monitor their battles to ensure compliance with the rules of war (see EZLN 2001a). But while all this is significant, what would truly distinguish the Zapatistas as rebels is the novel, creative and innovative path to radical social change they would embark on in the days after the uprising — a path grounded in democracy, dialogue, inclusivity and the mutual recognition of dignity. This path — and its significance to others within and outside of Mexico — is what I trace in the chapters to come.

Twelve days in January

In the early hours of 1 January 1994, the Zapatista Army of National Liberation exploded onto the political horizon at national and even global levels. As the North American Free Trade Agreement came into effect, 5,000 Zapatista insurgents led by 130 officers — almost exclusively young indigenous men and women — emerged from ten years of clandestine organizing and five centuries of indigenous resistance to colonization, genocide and exploitation, and declared war against the federal executive, represented by President Carlos Salinas de Gortari, and the Mexican federal army (Womack 1999: 42). Equipped with rubber boots and homemade uniforms, their faces concealed by bandanas and balaclavas, their weapons ranging from semi-automatic machine guns to single-shot .22 calibre rifles and toy guns carved from wood, the insurgents of the EZLN seized towns, cities and ranches across eastern and central Chiapas (Collier and Quaratiello 1999: 1). Leaving 4,000 fighters behind as a rearguard, the 5,000 EZLN insurgents took control of seven cities in the highlands of Chiapas: San Cristóbal de las Casas, Ocosingo, Las Margaritas, Altamirano, Chanal, Oxchuc and Huixtán (Harvey 1998: 6; Womack 199: 42). While Zapatista troops engaged agents of state security from local police forces to the federal army during the course of the uprising, the EZLN was remarkable from the outset with regard to the restraint demonstrated by its insurgent fighters and its careful avoidance of civilian casualties.

From the main balconies of the municipal halls in each occupied city, Zapatista commanders read the 'First Declaration of the Lacandón Jungle', the Zapatista declaration of war, which was also distributed to the Mexican people through a small newspaper called *El Despertador Mexicano* (The Mexican Awakener) (Muñoz Ramírez 2008: 105–6). Explaining the gross injustices at the root of the rebellion, the first Zapatista declaration outlined the main points animating the struggle: work, land, shelter, bread, health, education, democracy, liberty, peace, independence and justice (Ross 2000: 20). The declaration also expressed the EZLN's goal to advance on Mexico City, defeat the federal army, depose the president and allow all Mexicans to select their own leaders freely and democratically (see EZLN 2001a).

If the EZLN's offensive was a tremendous success on the first day of the new year, 2 January brought a drastic change of fortune. The EZLN's original battle plans had involved four operations conducted by four separate forces with general battle orders to advance as far as possible (Womack 1999: 42). However, the regiment assigned to impede the Mexican army forces on the road from Palenque to Ocosingo could not even slow the advancing units down and the EZLN forces assigned to take Ocosingo were therefore caught unprepared and surrounded by 3,400 Mexican government troops (Womack 1999: 43; Muñoz Ramírez 2008: 107). While the rebel seizure of San Cristóbal de las Casas — the old colonial capital of the state — was a dramatic highlight of the uprising, Ocosingo was a nightmare. Indeed, the battle in Ocosingo between government forces and Zapatista insurgents would continue for two days and would be the most brutal and bloody of the uprising. With instructions to have 'no compunction about summary executions', government forces fought Zapatista forces first in the Ocosingo marketplace and, later, from house to house, ensuring an abundance of civilian casualties (Ross 2000: 24). While the EZLN sought to avoid civilian casualties, government forces did not show similar restraint. Surviving Zapatista troops ultimately abandoned Ocosingo and retreated into the canyons of Chiapas.

Outside of San Cristóbal de las Casa, another critical battle occurred on 2 January. EZLN battle plans had not only included the cutting off of government troops from Palenque to Ocosingo — a move that had utterly failed — but also hinged upon a successful assault against the headquarters of the 31st Military Zone at Rancho Nuevo just outside of San Cristóbal (Womack 1999: 42–3). Pinning down the soldiers at the base was a tactical necessity in order to cover the withdrawal of Zapatista troops from the cities they had briefly occupied. Taking the base was the ultimate prize, however, because it meant access to needed weapons and ammunition. So as the Zapatista forces abandoned San Cristóbal on 2 January they descended upon Rancho Nuevo, attempting to pin down government troops and cover the retreat of other Zapatista units, liberate weapons and ammunition and defeat the base if possible (Ross 2000: 25–6). While the EZLN did not succeed in capturing the base, the insurgents did manage to keep the federal army soldiers restricted to it, as well as liberating a cache of automatic weapons and grenades (26). After this, the insurgents retreated into the jungle once more. As the Zapatistas retreated, one unit, headed by Mayor Moisés, stopped to take General Absalón Castellanos Domínguez into custody (27). The general had been the governor of Chiapas from 1982 until 1988, earning a reputation for repression and brutality, and he was now a Zapatista prisoner of war. Castellanos would eventually be released by the EZLN in exchange for hundreds of indigenous Zapatistas who had been detained and tortured in state prisons. As Gloria Muñoz Ramírez, a Mexican journalist and long-time Zapatista correspondent, explains:

> The act of freeing the former governor of Chiapas was not only the exchange of a cruel and heartless prisoner of war for hundreds of

jailed indigenous Zapatistas. It was also the ethical debut of an insurgent movement that instead of sacrificing the ex-governor accused
of various assassinations, condemned him to carry the forgiveness
of those whom he had despised, humiliated and exploited over so
many years. (Muñoz Ramírez 2008: 117)

This powerful ethico-political statement would prefigure the
kinds of inspiring and creative political innovation the Zapatistas
would produce over the coming years.

As the Zapatista insurgents retreated back into the canyons and
jungle of Chiapas, the federal army moved in, establishing the familiar geography of 'low-intensity warfare'. Familiar to other parts
of Latin America and around the world in situations where state
forces confront an insurgency with popular, grassroots support,
low-intensity warfare is a euphemism for a form of conflict in
which the state and its agents aim to disrupt the social fabric
upon which an insurgency relies. In other words, in situations of
low-intensity warfare, it is the civilian population of a region that
comes to be targeted by military and paramilitary forces. While
state forces may choose to use 'carrots' — such as distributing
food or medicine — to win local support, by far the more common
characteristics of this form of warfare involve the use of 'sticks'
to undermine rebel support — setting up military checkpoints to
disrupt people's movements, harassing and intimidating the local
population, arming paramilitary groups, arbitrarily detaining
people, and generally making daily life as difficult and fear-ridden
as possible. As tens of thousands of Mexican federal army troops
flooded into Chiapas, this is the landscape that began to take
shape. If the Zapatista uprising had followed the conventional
storyline established by so many other failed insurgencies in
Latin America, this moment should have signalled a descent into
a bloody, terror-filled and protracted conflict. As would become
clear, however, the Zapatistas are anything but conventional.

While the EZLN was being driven back into the jungles of Chiapas by the force of the Mexican federal army's counter-attack, news of the uprising had spread well beyond Chiapas and, indeed, far beyond Mexico. As the federal army began indiscriminately bombing the hills around San Cristóbal de las Casas and areas in the jungle in a desperate attempt to strike back at the insurgents, ordinary people both within and outside of Mexico with no pre-existing links to the Zapatistas began to mobilize to bring an end to the fighting. While federal army forces were moving aggressively against the retreating EZLN forces, important events were also unfolding far away from Chiapas in the halls of power in Mexico City. President Salinas moved quickly to fire his minister of the interior – and former governor of Chiapas — Patrocinio González and to replace him with current ombudsman of the National Human Rights Commission, Jorge Carpizo (Ross 2000: 32). In addition to this, on 10 January Salinas appointed Manuel Camacho Solís, former mayor of Mexico City, to become the government's Commissioner of Peace and Reconciliation in Chiapas (32). Combined with Salinas's desire to legislate an amnesty for rebels who chose to lay down their arms, these two appointments signalled the government's desire to pursue a policy of engagement — however insincere — rather than annihilation with respect to the EZLN (Womack 1999: 44).

Parallel to this, Mexican civil society was already moving to bring about an end to the conflict. Historian John Womack, Jr eloquently summarizes the spirit animating Mexican civil society in the first days of 1994:

A public hoping through NAFTA to establish itself in 'the First World' suddenly had to recognize how deeply a part of 'The Third World' it also remained. To their immense credit, within a few days, amid stupefying confusion and bewildering denunciations right, left, and center, most Mexicans outside Chiapas formed two clear, simple opinions: they were for the poor Indians in Chiapas, and they were against war. (1999: 44)

The Association of Civil Organizations for Peace (CONPAZ) was one of the first organizations formed by civic organizations in Mexico in an attempt to reign in the military and bring an end to the fighting (Muñoz Ramírez 2008: 110). As grassroots support for their struggle, if not the means, grew, the EZLN issued a communiqué proposing the conditions by which it would consent to negotiations with the government: recognition as a belligerent force, a ceasefire on both sides, the withdrawal of federal troops, an end to the bombing, and the formation of a National Commission of Intermediation (110). As protests in solidarity with the Zapatistas spread throughout Mexico and around the world, the Salinas government found itself faced with an increasingly untenable war in Chiapas.

The final straw for the government came on 12 January 1994, as a massive protest in support of the Zapatistas and calling for an end to the war and the initiation of negotiations was planned for the Zócalo (central square) of Mexico City. With more than 100,000 people packing the Zócalo and demanding an end to the war, Salinas called for a unilateral ceasefire and for negotiations with the insurgents (Muñoz Ramírez 2008: 112). The precise count of those killed, wounded and disappeared over the course of the Zapatistas' initial uprising remains uncertain, particularly because the Mexican federal army closed the conflict zone to journalists and other observers. Available reports present different numbers while painting a coherent overall picture, one marked by significant abuses and an extreme and indiscriminate use of violence by the Mexican federal army. At the end of five days of combat, the Zapatistas issued the following report: 9 Zapatistas dead, 20 badly wounded; for the Mexican Army, 27 dead, 40 wounded, and 180 prisoners who had surrendered and had later been freed (109). In its 1993–94 report, the Mexican National Human Rights Commission counted 207 dead: 16 federal soldiers; 38 civilian security agents; 67 civilians; 48 Zapatista insurgents; and 38 unidentified bodies (Ross 2000: 33). The Commission also claimed that of the 427 civilians reported missing during the conflict, 407 had been located by February 1994 (33). Contradicting the Commission, the Diocese of San Cristóbal de las Casas claimed 400 dead, suggesting that the Mexican federal army had disposed of many of the bodies in order to conceal evidence of its 'excesses' during the uprising (33). John Womack, Jr offers the following accounting of the dead: 13 Mexican army soldiers; 38 state police; more than 70 Zapatistas; and 'from 19 to 275 or more civilians' (1999: 43–4).

While the ceasefire would hardly mark the end of violence in Chiapas, 12 January would signal the beginning of an entirely new phase of the Zapatista struggle — one hinging upon communication and engagement with civil societies nationally and globally. As Zapatista spokesperson and military commander Subcomandante Insurgente Marcos would remark, 'We did not go to war on January 1 to kill or to have them kill us. We went to make ourselves heard' (Womack 1999: 44). The rest of this book is a critical introduction to this complex, hopeful and creative political dialogue initiated by the Zapatistas with a diversity of others both near and far as they have sought to build a world marked by dignity, justice, democracy, liberty and peace.

Masks and Marcos

When Zapatista forces took control of San Cristóbal de las Casas on 1 January, one of the first questions they were asked is why they masked their faces with balaclavas or bandanas. To this question, a Zapatista officer who identified himself by the *nom de guerre* 'Subcomandante Insurgente Marcos' replied that the Zapatistas wore masks for two reasons:

> The primary one is that we have to watch out for protagonism — in other words, that people do not promote themselves too much. It is about being anonymous, not because we fear for ourselves, but rather so that they cannot corrupt us. ... We know that our leadership is collective and that we have to submit to them. Even though you happen to be listening to me now because I am here, in other places others, masked in the same way, are talking. This masked person today is called Marcos here and tomorrow will be called Pedro in Margaritas or José in Ocosingo or Alfredo in Altamirano or whatever he is called. Finally, the one who speaks is a more collective heart, not a caudillo [a charismatic, personalistic leader]. That is what I want you to understand, not a caudillo in the old style, in that image. The only image that you will have is that those who make this happen are masked. And the time will come when the people will realize that it is enough to have dignity and put on a mask and say: Well then, I can do this too. (2002a: 209–10)

In addition to the reasons outlined by Marcos above, the masked faces of the Zapatista insurgents were also meant to evoke the status of indigenous peoples in Mexico. By masking themselves the Zapatistas became faceless, anonymous, without identity. The denial of dignity — and all the consequences that flow from that act — has long been a characteristic of the fate imposed upon indigenous peoples following the invasion of the Americas by Europeans. Without faces and without dignity, entire peoples became fodder for colonialism, imperialism, moderniz-ation, and capitalism. By taking up the mask voluntarily, the Zapatistas reclaimed the dignity stolen from indigenous peoples by reminding the world that the most marginalized, most invis-ible, most oppressed had the power to remake their world. As the Zapatistas asserted, by masking their faces and taking up arms those most marginalized within the 'New World Order' of global neoliberal capitalism insisted that the world take notice of them once again.

The mask — whether balaclava or bandana — has become an icon of the Zapatista movement. Ironically, so too has the man who explained the Zapatistas' use of the mask to counter the emergence of a cult of personality around singular figures in what is indisputably a collective and grassroots movement. Standing a foot taller than his indigenous comrades, wearing a short black serape, his chest criss-crossed by bandoliers of shotgun shells, Subcomandante Marcos facilitated the introduction of the EZLN to curious locals, tourists, and the rest of Mexico and the world on the first day of the new year in 1994. Explaining that he was one of the very few non-indigenous members of the EZLN and that he was a *subcomandante* — subcommander — bound to obey the orders of the Clandestine Revolutionary Indigenous Committee, the General Command of the EZLN, Marcos stepped into his role as a conduit and key communicator for the Zapatista struggle with the world beyond the indigenous communities of Chiapas.

Marcos's stellar communicative abilities were immediately apparent. Speaking several languages — including Spanish and local Mayan dialects — Marcos had a communicative capacity that extended well beyond a proficiency at learning language. Indeed, as the Zapatista struggle unfolded in the days after the occupation of San Cristóbal, Marcos's extraordinary literary flair would become well known within Mexico and around the world. Abandoning the bureaucratic language of past revolutionary movements in favour of myth-making, poetry, philosophical inquiries, incisive analysis, irony, satire and endless argumentation, Marcos's communiqués have been reprinted in local and national newspapers, have circulated the world via the Internet, and have been republished as edited volumes. All too frequently misidentified as *the leader* of the Zapatista insurgency, a lazy claim unsupported by any serious analysis of the organizational history of the EZLN and one smacking of racism, Marcos has nevertheless been a vital conduit of communication between the EZLN and the wider world, a brilliant political strategist, and a central icon for the alter-globalization movement.

But who *is* Subcomandante Insurgente Marcos? The answer to this question is not straightforward. In February 1995, the Mexican federal government decided it had uncovered the 'truth' of Marcos's identity. Not coincidentally, 1995 marked the dramatic devaluation of the Mexican peso. As explained to the Mexican nation by Finance Minister Jaime Serra Puche on live television, the devaluation was necessary 'in order to confront uncertainties that have been generated by the conflict in Chiapas' (Ross 2000: 97). The explanation of the devaluation of the peso by 15 per cent, an economic policy aimed at encouraging foreign investment in Mexico as well as the exportation of suddenly cheaper Mexican goods, appeared to be a tacit government admission of the influence wielded by the EZLN over economic policy (97). In reality, the Mexican economy had been in a downward spiral for some time due to the poor financial decisions made, in particular, by the previous government of Carlos Salinas (98). With Mexico about to default on $17 billion in loans, domestic and foreign investors, taking full advantage of the capital mobility afforded by neoliberal globalization, pulled their money out of Mexico, effectively crashing the economy (98). The US government under Bill Clinton threw the Zedillo government in Mexico a lifeline, extending the largest bailout loan in history in order to rescue the United States' new NAFTA partner. With the economy ravaged but stabilized, the pressure was on the Zedillo government to demonstrate it had full control of its own national territory, not because the Zapatistas had precipitated the crash but because their very existence gave the lie to neoliberal mythology that global capitalism was a tide that would lift all boats.

To save face and in order to demonstrate his competence as president and commander-in-chief, President Zedillo prepared to move aggressively against the Zapatistas, violating the terms of the ceasefire and jeopardizing hope of renewed peace negotiations. Key to this new government offensive was the issuing of arrest warrants for the Zapatista leadership and, perhaps even more importantly, the 'unmasking' of Subcomandante Marcos. Since the first days of the uprising, Marcos had become a larger-than-life figure, an icon of the Zapatista movement, and his romantic revolutionary allure was only deepened by his concealed identity. Unmasking Marcos was key to the government's attempts to demobilize support for the Zapatistas. In a press conference on 9 February 1995, Zedillo revealed to the Mexican nation the man Mexican intelligence services believed Marcos to be: Rafael Sebastián Guillén Vicente, a native of Tampico, Tamaulipas and a former university professor (Ross 2000: 108). During the press conference, a government aide displayed a photograph of Guillén — an unremarkable looking man with a beard and large, dark eyes (Guillermoprieto 2002: 33). Over the photograph, the aide superimposed a slide of a balaclava, thus masking and unmasking the man the government claimed was Marcos (33). Guillén was a philosophy graduate of the National Autonomous University of Mexico, located in Mexico City, and his thesis focused on the work of Louis Althusser, the French Structural Marxist (Ross 2000: 108). Indeed, some observers have commented on the stylistic similarities between Guillén's writing and Marcos's communiqués (see Guillermoprieto 2002: 37; Ross 2000: 108). Later, Guillén became a professor at the Autonomous Metropolitan University's Xochimilco campus, a place with a reputation for radicalism and social activism (Guillermoprieto 2002: 36). Guillén, who taught in the Design Science and Arts Division, is remembered by those who knew him as 'brilliant, serious, and hard-working', a 'brilliant orator', a 'congenial' person of 'great solidarity' with a 'good sense of humor' (Guillermoprieto 2002: 36; Ross 2000: 108).

Ultimately, the government's attempt to arrest the Zapatista leadership was an abysmal failure, as was its attempt to demystify Marcos. In response to the 'unmasking' and Zedillo's renewed offensive against the Zapatistas, Mexican civil society organized huge demonstrations in Mexico City's Zócalo (Ross 2000: 109). At the demonstrations, crowds of more than 100,000 people responded to Zedillo's 'unmasking' by chanting '¡Todos somos Marcos!' — 'We are all Marcos!' (109). This statement not only expressed a deep solidarity with the Zapatistas but also embodied the central point behind the Zapatistas use of the mask. As rebels who had masked themselves 'in order to be seen', armed themselves 'in order to be heard', the Zapatistas — and the figure of Marcos in particular — had become symbols of the struggles of all those marginalized, oppressed and exploited by dominant political and economic systems.

For his own part, Marcos wasted little time in responding to his supposed unmasking. In a communiqué entitled 'The Retreat Is Making Us Almost Scratch the Sky', written and issued as the Zapatista leadership retreated from the government offensive, Marcos addresses the issue of his identity in a 'P.S.' to the communiqué taking the form of a mock trial:

> P.S. ... WHICH APPOINTS ITSELF 'special investigator on the Sup's case,' and invites the national and international civic society to be the jury and to pronounce the sentence. Being such and such an hour, on such and such a day, of such and such a month, in the current year, standing before this P.S. is a man of indefinite age, between five and

sixty-five years old, his face covered with one of those garments that appears to be a sock with holes in it (and which the gringos call a ski mask, and Latin Americans call pasa-montañas). There are two visible features on the face, one which, after several sneezes, we deduce is the nose. The other, judging by the emanations of smoke and the smell of tobacco, could be a pipe, like the ones used by sailors, intellectuals, pirates, and fugitives from justice. Sworn to say the truth and nothing but the truth, the individual in question says his name is 'Marcos Montes de la Selva,' son of Old Don Antonio and Doña Juanita, brother to young Antonio, Ramona, and Susana, uncle to Toñita, Beto, Eva, and Heriberto [all indigenous Zapatistas who appear in communiqués written by Marcos]. Speaking before me, he declares himself to be in full use of his physical and mental faculties, and without any pressure (other than the 60,000 federal soldiers who are looking for him dead or alive) states and confesses the following:

First. That he was born in the guerrilla camp called Agua Fria, in the Lacandon Jungle, Chiapas, early one morning in August 1984, and that he was reborn 1 January 1994, and reborn, successively, on June 10, 1994, on August 8, 1994, the nineteenth of December 1994, the tenth of February 1995, and each day and each hour and each minute and each second since that day up to this moment, in which I am making this statement. (Subcomandante Marcos 2001C: 228–9)

The interrogation continues, with Marcos brilliantly making use of the scenario to illustrate the inherent justness of the Zapatista struggle as well as the deep rootedness of the identity of 'Marcos' within that struggle. He concludes the interrogation in compelling fashion, blowing apart the very notion of fixed identities and utterly mocking the 'unmasking' that the Zedillo government had worked so hard to engineer while illustrating the provocative nature of the Zapatista challenge to conventional politics:

The owner of the voice confesses that he was completely bored with this interrogation. This earned him a severe reprimand from the P.S.

interrogator, who explained to him that the case will continue until the supreme government finds another tale with which to entertain itself.

After these confessions, the owner of the voice was exhorted to spontaneously declare himself innocent or guilty of the following series of accusations. To each accusation, the owner of the voice responded:

The whites accuse him of being dark. Guilty.
The dark ones accuse him of being white. Guilty.
The authentic accuse him of being indigenous. Guilty.
The treasonous indigenous accuse him of being *mestizo*. Guilty.
The machos accuse him of being feminine. Guilty.
The feminists accuse him of being macho. Guilty.
The communists accuse him of being anarchist. Guilty.
The anarchists accuse him of being orthodox. Guilty.
The Anglos accuse him of being Chicano. Guilty.
The anti-Semites accuse him of being pro-Jews. Guilty.
The Jews accuse him of being pro-Arab. Guilty.
The Europeans accuse him of being Asiatic. Guilty.
The government officials accuse him of being an opportunist. Guilty.
The reformists accuse him of being an extremist, a radical. Guilty.
The radicals accuse him of being reformist. Guilty.
The 'historical vanguard' accuse him of appealing to the civic society and not to the proletariat. Guilty.
The civic society accuses him of disturbing their tranquility. Guilty.
The Stock Exchange accuses him of ruining their breakfast. Guilty.
The government accuses him of increasing the consumption of antacids by government agencies. Guilty.
The serious ones accuse him of being a jokester. Guilty.
The adults accuse him of being a child. Guilty.
The children accuse him of being an adult. Guilty.
The orthodox leftists accuse him of not condemning the homosexuals and lesbians. Guilty.

The theoreticians accuse him of being a practitioner. Guilty.
The practitioners accuse him of being a theorist. Guilty.
Everyone accuses him of everything bad that has happened.
   Guilty. (Subcomandante Marcos: 231)

Confessing to be every troubling, marginalized, excluded
identity while insisting that he had been born in a guerrilla
camp in Chiapas in 1984 and reborn constantly since, Marcos
became nothing less than the quintessential rebel, a figure who
is always a myth and a provocation. In essence, Marcos denied
the significance of who he had been before the Zapatista struggle
began. As long as the movement continued, he could not be
'unmasked'.

As for the allegation that Marcos is really Rafael Sebastián
Guillén Vicente from Tampico, Marcos responded in another
communiqué that

I heard that they discovered another Marcos and he is very tampi-
queno [very much from Tampico]. It does not sound bad, the port is
beautiful. I remember when I was working as a bouncer in a brothel
in Ciudad Madero during the times in which La Quina did to the
regional economy what Salinas did to the stock exchange: to inject
money to hide poverty. I left the port because humidity makes me
sleepy, and seafood makes the sleepiness go away. (Subcomandante
Marcos 2004e: 86)

Playing with the attempted unmasking, refuting its significance
on the one hand while denying its claims on the other, Marcos
accomplished what he so often would throughout the course
of the Zapatista rebellion: to work imaginatively and creatively
while defying conventional political logic and the threat of defeat
to communicate Zapatismo as a rebel political philosophy and
practice emerging from the work of Zapatista insurgents and base
communities alike. If these attempts were not always successful
it is because articulating and living a political project aimed at

radical social transformation is not easy. That so many of these attempts have been successful — opening windows of political possibility for so many others both near and far — is a testament to the joy of rebellion and the passion for a life lived collectively with dignity that animate the Zapatista struggle.

1

'We are the product of
five hundred years of resistance'

THE ORIGINS OF ZAPATISMO

ALL MODERN nation-states in the Americas are products of the 'encounter' between European colonizers and the indigenous populations native to these territories. Of course, for these diverse indigenous peoples, this euphemistically termed 'encounter' between peoples marked the beginning of five centuries of genocide, racism, slavery, neglect, repression, and the denial of their capacity for self-determination and autonomy. These five centuries have also borne witness to indigenous resistance to this colonial project of domination and erasure and, more recently, to the resurgence of indigenous peoples and their cultures (see Alfred 2005). Despite these broad trends, it is important to recognize that in different parts of the Americas the project of colonial domination and nation-state building was realized very differently in relation to the existing indigenous inhabitants of these territories, and these differences deeply inform the way that indigenous projects of resistance and resurgence have been articulated. For example, while in Canada and the United States the project of nation-building was predicated upon the attempted erasure of the first peoples inhabiting these territories, in Mexico, as in much of Latin America, the nation-building project drew explicit links to its indigenous — albeit highly mythologized — past.

Throughout the Americas, the concrete effect of colonization was — and in many cases continues to be — massive violence directed against the peoples indigenous to these lands, but the distinction between nations like Canada and the United States seeking a radical break with what they sought to displace and occupy and those like Mexico seeking to lay claim to this indigenous legacy is not insignificant. Indeed, imagining the nation as a place linked to the indigenous civilizations that preceded it would provide a particular kind of symbolic currency for indigenous movements of resistance and resurgence to mobilize vis-à-vis the state, as well as situating them within a certain kind of context. In order to understand the contemporary Zapatista movement and the complex and creative dynamics of resistance and alternative-building enacted by it, it is first necessary to place it within this rich, complex and contradictory historical space. As such, it is to this historical intersection of indigenous struggle with rebellion, revolution and nation-building in Mexico that I now turn.

A struggle for independence
— by whom and for whom?

In the years following the Spanish invasion of Mesoamerica, indigenous peoples frequently sought ways — both 'legal' and 'extra-legal' — to resist Spanish rule (Cockcroft 1998: 35; see also Weinberg 2000). While the first acts of resistance often took the form of open warfare or flight, by the mid-1500s much of Mesoamerica had been militarily subdued by Spanish conquistadors while remaining a seedbed of rebellion waiting for any opportunity to erupt. Some of these acts of rebellion even made use of the Christian beliefs spread among — and often forced violently upon — indigenous peoples by Church missionaries to express their resistance. While the terms in which these acts of rebellion were expressed drew explicitly upon the religious system of the colonizers, this idiom was used to articulate demands that took direct aim at the colonial power structure, emphasized local autonomy, and defended local belief systems. An example of this is the Tzeltal Mayan Revolt which began in Chiapas in 1712 after a girl from the Tzeltal village of San Juan Cancuc claimed to have been visited by the Virgin Mary, who instructed the girl to build a chapel in her honour (Weinberg 2000: 23). When the villagers in Cancuc began the construction, they were ordered to be flogged by the local priest, who saw this as nothing less than devil worship (23). The Tzeltales resisted, driving the priest out and defying the authority of Spanish political and religious powers (23). Neighbouring villages sent people to Cancuc to be ordained in the new religious order even as they raised an indigenous army to confront their oppressors (23). Although the revolt was eventually put down, it stands as a testament to the spirit of indigenous rebellion and resistance which was never extinguished.

Of course, indigenous resistance to the new colonial order occurred for other reasons and on other terms. In 1847, Mexican dictator Santa Anna went to war with the United States over Texas, and the Yucatan declared independence from Mexico (Weinberg 2000: 25). The *ladino* — non-indigenous — elites in the Yucatan conscripted a Mayan army to fight for independence, buying loyalty with promises of land reform and the abolition of church dues, taxes, and debt labour. However, once the conscripts had been trained and armed, the *ladino* elite refused to honour the terms of the agreement and Mayan troops revolted (25).

The governor of the Yucatan executed the leaders of the revolt
— sparking a general Mayan rebellion known as the 'Caste War
of the Yucatan' that nearly succeeded in capturing the capital city
of the Yucatan and overthrowing the colonial power structure
before it was defeated in 1848 (26).

Following the rebellion, Yucatan elites sought to punish the
Maya for their defiance. Many Maya were forcibly relocated
further south into the Yucatan's interior, their crops uprooted,
even as Indian slavery was reinstated (Weinberg 2000: 26). Some
Maya who survived this attempt at annihilation found hope in
a cult of the 'talking cross' which emerged at a remote refugee
settlement known as Chan Santa Cruz. The Maya cultists called
themselves the 'Cruzob' — 'the Spanish word for cross with the
Maya plural suffix' — and they were immediately targeted as a
threat by Yucatan *ladino* elites (26). The Cruzob resisted and,
playing on the political turmoil that engulfed Mexico in the
mid-1800s, endured to constitute a significant threat to local and
federal control of the Yucatan interior (26–7). Eventually, the
Mexican federal army was brought in to deal with the Cruzob
challenge, but while it succeeded in taking Chan Santa Cruz, it
only drove the Cruzob deeper into the Yucatan interior where
they continued to launch raids against non-indigenous villages
and towns and to destroy projects aimed at building the state's
infrastructure (27). Indeed, it would not be until the 1930s and
the social, political, and economic reforms instituted by Mexico's
post-revolutionary regime that some of the grievances — such as
Indian slavery and land reform — animating the Cruzob War
would be at least partially addressed and the Cruzob themselves
effectively demobilized (28).

These examples illustrate the militant, armed face of indigenous
resistance to colonial elites and their power structures. They are
significant because they stand as testaments to the enduring spirit

of indigenous defiance to colonial domination that could never be completely repressed. However, while resistance often took the form of open and armed rebellion, indigenous peoples also sought to resist Spanish plunder of their lands through Indian legislation which 'declared respect for the territorial patrimony of indigenous peoples' (Warman 1976: 29). While largely rhetorical and rarely respected, the colonial recognition of indigenous rights would prove foundational for the way that the nascent Mexican state and indigenous struggles would be positioned in relation to one another.

Beginning in 1810, indigenous resistance to colonial domination and popular struggles for Mexican independence from Spain would increasingly cross paths. Often remembered from a nationalist perspective as a 'Mexican' rejection of Spanish domination and a struggle for independence, the popular rebellion unleashed in Mexico during the Wars of Independence was, in fact, a complex and contradictory phenomenon. The independence movement comprised at least three distinct elements: the first, commercial–industrial–agricultural elites interested in gaining control over the 'bureaucratic pivot' of Mexico City; the second, elements in rebellion against 'centralized officialdom' of the colonial state; the third, actors seeking to realize a regime of social justice (Wolf 1969: 7–8). Representatives of this third element, Father Miguel Hidalgo and Father José María Morelos, raised peasant armies in opposition to the abuses and excesses of the colonial state and its masters (Cockcroft 1998: 55). The commitment to social justice was particularly evident in the insurrectionary leadership provided by Father Morelos. On 17 November 1810, Morelos proclaimed an end to discrimination, institutionalized racism, slavery and Indian tribute, as well as calling for a return of the lands stolen from indigenous peoples to them (Wolf 1969: 8). However, as soon as it became clear to Mexican elites that this rebellion was aimed not only at the Spanish Crown but at their own entrenched privilege in pursuit of a regime of social justice, the army, the Church and the powerful landholding families quickly came to the defence of the Spanish Crown and crushed the rebellion (9). Following this trajectory, independence from Spain would ultimately be won for Mexico in 1821 by elites seeking to protect their own advantage and wealth in the face of a liberalizing Spanish constitution. The revolutionary struggle for independence animated by social justice principles and mobilized by Fathers Hidalgo and Morelos was thus both exploited and ultimately crushed by an opportunistic and self-interested elite, a dynamic which not for the last time would characterize mass struggle in Mexico.

Following Mexico's elite-engineered independence from Spain, Chiapas was annexed by Mexico. Much like the national move to independence, the annexation of Chiapas from Guatemala was an elite-driven event aimed at preserving their commercial interests and maintaining their domination of indigenous labour (Benjamin 1996: 11). Much like the intra-elite power struggles beginning to play themselves out in central Mexico, following Chiapas's annexation, two elite factions began to struggle against each other over the control of land and labour (13). Located in the Central Highlands and the Central Valley respectively, these two factions became linked to the struggle that was playing itself out in central Mexico. Aligning themselves with liberalism, the farmers and ranchers of the valleys challenged the power of the highland heirs of the colonial oligarchy who — along with their allies in traditional sources of power and authority like the Church — identified with conservatism (13). Ideological differences aside, in Chiapas the primary prize at stake was the control and exploitation of the indigenous population and their labour (14). Nevertheless, as Chiapanecan elites came to identify with the liberal/conservative polarization of central Mexico, the significance of the national struggle which would explode in the 1850s and after increased dramatically.

The double-edged sword of modernization

The next chapter in the history of revolution in Mexico would take place in the 1850s. While the dictator Santa Anna had successfully managed to hold on to power by repressing, jailing, or executing his political challengers, he met his match in liberal leaders such as Benito Juárez backed by anti-government rebels in Guerrero (Cockcroft 1998: 70–71). Faced with this opposition, Santa Anna ceded power and sailed into exile, but while this act of power changing elite hands by no means signified lasting social peace in Mexico, it did entail some profound consequences. Once in power, the triumphant liberals ushered in the Liberal Reform, abolishing clerical and military special privileges and forbidding any 'corporation' from owning property (71). This liberal modernization of Mexican political, social and economic relationships enraged conservatives, yet the abolition of 'corporately held property' affected not only powerful institutions like the Church but peasant and indigenous communities as well. Ejidos, communally-held and worked land, were also a form of 'corporately held property' and their legal dissolution represented a profound challenge to traditional forms of peasant landholding (71). The first response to this liberalization of economic, political and social relationships came in a reactionary form as Mexican conservatives invited French military intervention against the liberal threat to their power and privilege. The result of this direct intervention was the installation of Mexico's new 'emperor', Austrian Archduke Maximilian, an imposition that resulted in civil war from 1862 until 1867 (72).

In order to finance their war against their conservative op-
ponents and French invasion, the liberals accelerated the pace of
land expropriation. The targets of this expropriation were largely
indigenous, as they often could not 'prove' their ownership of
the land (Cockcroft 1998: 72). While the Reform Laws were
intended to 'free the individual from traditional fetters', they
succeeded only in introducing new forms of bondage to the lives
of people who already faced multiple forms of domination and
exploitation (Wolf 1969: 13). In the words of Eric Wolf, 'Freedom
for the landowner would mean freedom to acquire more land to
add to his already engorged holdings; freedom for the Indian
— no longer subject to his community and now lord of his own
property — would mean the ability to sell his land, and to join
the throng of landless in search of employment' (13). While
the liberal Reform Laws effectively challenged certain powerful
actors and their entrenched privilege, they also represented a
new front in the assault upon indigenous lifeways in the name
of 'progress'.

Far from the power struggles animating central Mexico, in
Chiapas 'modernization' took on very particular dimensions in
relation to indigenous communities. As a result of the Reform
Laws, indigenous indebted servitude became 'one of the faces
of … "progress" in the 1870s and 1880s' (Benjamin 1996: 28).
Ironically, 'revolution' or claims to progressive reform for Chiapanecos would all too often come to signify new and even more
pervasive forms of domination and exploitation as the individual
was 'freed' from the bonds of community to sell his labour on the
open market. Ultimately, the radical destabilization that would
result from this liberal–conservative conflict would culminate in
the Mexican Revolution. In another sadly ironic twist, even as
liberal and conservative elites sought to consolidate their privilege
and power by pillaging the most vulnerable, the war against the

French invaders was fought and won largely by peasants and workers engaged in guerrilla struggle (Cockcroft 1998: 75).

Revolution on the horizon

The liberal victory over the conservatives and their French allies secured neither peace nor prosperity in Mexico. What it did do, however, was to set the stage for the Mexican Revolution in 1910. Made vulnerable by debt, feuding and internal strife, in 1876 the liberal 'bourgeois-democratic' state gave way to an 'oligarchic-dictatorial' one led by General Porfirio Díaz (Cockcroft 1998: 81). During his 35-year rule, which ended only when the Revolution deposed him in 1911, Díaz would pursue the liberal modernization project for Mexico. Practically, this meant building industry and elite wealth on the backs of the peasantry and workers and brutally silencing opposition (81). Known as the 'Científicos' (scientists) due to their self-identification as positivist scientists pursuing Mexico's modernization through the application of enlightened knowledge and 'natural law', Díaz and his inner circle of advisors conceived of this project as one made possible only through the obliteration of the nation's indigenous element and the 'further-ance of "white" control, national or international' (Wolf 1969: 14). True to the spirit of an age that managed to combine 'scientific enlightenment' with racist theories of 'progress' and the 'civiliz-ing' mission of colonial and imperial domination, under Díaz's paternalistic control, Juárez's liberal reform became a nightmare of modernization for indigenous peoples as it sought to under-mine the few remaining bases of social and political autonomy afforded to them.

Under the charismatic and coercive leadership of Porfirian gov-ernors such as Emilio Rabasa and his successors, Chiapas would become 'one of the laboratories of modernization' (Benjamin

1996: 34). While modernization meant many things in Chiapas, including the building of transportation and communications infrastructure and the implementation of 'modern' techniques to everything from schooling to farming, perhaps its most significant manifestation was its goal of 'transforming Indians into yeoman farmers, free laborers, and Mexicans' (33). Modernization thus came to represent the obliteration of all that was 'backward' — that is, all that was indigenous. Through Governor Rabasa's programme of agrarian reform known as *el reparto*, the state sought to increase the number of small farmers and property owners in accordance with modern notions of development and progress. Under this program the assault on village *ejidos* only intensified (49). New forms of labour exploitation emerged and intensified as indigenous communities lost access to and control over their own lands. Indigenous peoples were forced into systems of 'indebted servitude, temporary migrant labor, and slave labor', with those not tied to large estates by debt working as day-wage labourers, sharecroppers or renters (89). The modernist dream of Mexican elites seemed to be proceeding perfectly, with indigenous peoples 'freed' from the shackles of tradition now free to sell their labour in exchange for survival.

In spite of the massive disruption of the social fabric caused by Díaz's project of modernization — underwritten by a racist imagination of 'progress' — coupled with the blatantly anti-democratic nature of his regime, it would not be until the beginning of the twentieth century that the makings of a serious challenge to Díaz would begin to coalesce. Known as the Precursor Movement to the Mexican Revolution, the Partido Liberal Mexicano (PLM, Mexican Liberal Party) was officially organized in 1905. The PLM grew out of hundreds of 'Liberal Clubs' formed at the beginning of the century by disaffected bourgeois liberals and intellectuals who baulked at the Díaz regime's authoritarianism and its concessions to the Church (Cockcroft 1998: 91). Anarchist organizers Ricardo and Enrique Flores Magón and Antonio Díaz Soto y Gama worked to radicalize these Liberal Clubs, and in 1906 the PLM officially turned itself into a political-military organization motivated by a radical anti-imperial ideology strongly in favour of the working class, peasants and progressive elements of the upper classes, drawing tens of thousands of Mexicans to its cause (91). Rather than a reformist organization, the PLM represents the emergence of a strong anarcho-revolutionary thread within the larger Mexican revolutionary tradition, a thread that would be profoundly informative for the way future radical struggles such as that of the Zapatistas would articulate themselves.

From 1906 to 1910 the PLM organized strikes and even armed uprisings against the Díaz regime, actions that were ruthlessly and bloodily confronted by the military (Cockcroft 1998: 92). While peasants and workers organized through the PLM were massacred by the military for demonstrating their opposition to Díaz's regime, northern industrialists were chafing against a regime which they felt had ceased to serve their interests. When Díaz sought to extend his reign for yet another term in 1910, these northern elites rallied behind one of their own — Francisco Madero — as their choice for president (95). In the face of an increasingly mobilized and radicalized movement from below, revolution became a tool for northern elites to ensure that their interests would achieve primacy once again. In exile in the United States after escaping from prison where he had been put by Díaz, Madero issued his Plan of San Luis Potosí calling for a general insurrection against the Díaz regime (96). Madero would not even lead an army to victory in the war against the Díaz regime. Instead, Díaz would be toppled by the PLM and Pancho Villa's and Emiliano Zapata's armies. It is to the story of Emiliano Zapata and his Liberating Army of the South that I now turn in order to explain why marginalized groups would risk rising up in arms against the powerful Porfirian regime and what this mobilization would mean for future generations of radicals in Mexico.

Land and liberty: Zapata and the Mexican Revolution

Emiliano Zapata was born on 8 August 1879 in the village of San Miguel Anenecuilco in the state of Morelos (Gilly 2005: 62). Born into a peasant line with deep roots in the area, Zapata had ancestors who fought in both the Independence and Reform wars (62). Inheriting a small amount of land and livestock, Zapata was neither rich nor poor by local standards, but the relatively poor quality of his land led him to become involved in the animal trade and he established an impressive reputation for himself as an equine expert, particularly in the area of horse-breaking (62). Zapata's early years were spent sharecropping as well as training, buying and selling horses (Stephen 2002: 36). One particularly compelling story about Zapata's early years is that, after seeing his father reduced to tears as he watched the village orchard enclosed by the local hacienda, Emiliano promised that he would restore these lands to the village (36). True or not, this story certainly reflects the spirit that would animate Zapata's commitments as he grew to adulthood.

Anenecuilco was a largely indigenous village which had fought for years against the encroachment of local haciendas upon their lands. Emiliano Zapata grew up within this tradition and often found himself in conflict with officials and hacienda owners in his attempt to defend community land (Huizer 1970: 376). By the time he reached 30, Zapata had established a solid reputation for himself among the local peasantry on the basis of his own activity as well as his family history (Gilly 2005: 62). Elected head of the village defence committee on 12 September 1909, Zapata began his tenure by retaking communal lands seized by local haciendas and redistributing it to the villagers after legal channels had failed (Huizer 1970: 377). This example illustrates both the immediate impetus for and deeper driving force of the original Zapatismo. The first objective of struggle was to recover communal lands that had been appropriated by wealthy landowners (Gilly 2005: 63; see also Warman 1976: 93). The deeper logic to this struggle, however, was much more expansive and powerful than this. In the words of Adolfo Gilly, 'it was a true insurrection against all the forms of oppression, repression, plunder, and exploitation intensified by capitalist development' (2005: 63). At first, this insurrectionary spirit lacked a clear revolutionary program so it required something else to orbit around — a basic, intelligible demand that laid bare the gross injustice of the current system. While it is easy to see a reformist or even conservative orientation in the claims by peasants for the restoration of lost land, the struggle for the reclamation of communal lands appropriated by wealthy landowners with government complicity starkly illuminated the justness of revolutionary — and armed — action on the part of the dispossessed (63).

The implementation of the Reform Laws, the expansion of haciendas, the accelerating exploitation of the rural population, and the brutality and intransigence of wealthy landowners in the face of even moderate demands made by the peasantry ultimately prepared the terrain for more militant action (Huizer 1970: 398). Indeed, one of the things that makes the history of Emiliano Zapata and the Liberating Army of the South so compelling is that Zapata's army was made up not of professionalized forces but of campesinos themselves. The struggle of these original Zapatistas was thus a struggle for their very lives, a struggle

grounded in the daily oppressions and injustices they faced at
the hands of wealthy landowners within a system tailored to their
economic exploitation and political domination. This dynamic
within Mexican revolutionary history — that of communities
compelled to take radical action in order to defend themselves
from the imposition of an externally imposed oblivion — is one
that would repeat itself time and again but nowhere more spectacularly than on 1 January 1994.

While northern elites spoke grandly but acted ineffectually
against the regime of Porfirio Díaz, rebellion broke out among
peasant groups like Zapata's. Since Madero's Plan of San Luis
Potosí included a clause involving demands of an agrarian nature,
the northern elites managed to forge an alliance between themselves and an explosive peasantry that overthrew the Díaz regime
in less than four months (Warman 1976: 94). With Díaz in exile
and Mexico preparing for its first new president in thirty-five
years, Madero moved to disarm the various revolutionary groups
that had been so instrumental in defeating the Porfiriato. While
Madero sought to buy peace with the insurgent peasants of
Morelos at the price of democracy, Zapata's army 'did not want
the vote in the first place; they wanted access to the land' (96).
Defying elite attempts at co-optation these radicalized campesinos
occupied land and entered into direct conflict with the ascendant
elite, who, needless to say, hardly embraced the radical agrarian
demands of the Zapatistas (96). As northern elites worked to
craft a post-revolutionary regime that would satisfy their interests,
they sent General Victoriano Huerta and elements of the Mexican
army into Morelos on a punitive mission. In the face of this threat,
the Zapatistas declared their 'counter-revolution' against Madero's
'revolution', becoming a truly autonomous revolutionary movement (96). In fact, autonomy is a thread that ran deeply through
the Zapatista struggle during the Mexican Revolution. While

Zapata was known as the 'Caudillo' — the leader — 'of the South',
the regional commanders and their troops operating under his
banner owed him only nominal allegiance, always maintaining
their autonomy and often acting independently (Weinberg 2000:
49). For the Zapatistas — then as now — gaining access to the
levers of a corrupt and dominating power structure was never
the aim of their revolutionary struggle. Instead, the roots of the
revolution lay in land, autonomy, and justice — principles that
could not be won or simply given through participation in a
morally bankrupt game of power politics.

Emiliano Zapata signed and issued the Plan of Ayala in the
village of Ayala on 22 November 1911. The Plan was issued in an
effort to clarify to the rest of the Mexican nation why the Zapatistas
had not yet laid down their arms (Huizer 1970: 382). Beginning
with a complete rejection of Madero, the Plan proceeds to lay out
the fundamental tenets of Zapatismo. Particularly significant are
Articles 6, 7 and 8 which directly address the redistribution of
land to those who work it as well as the nationalization of lands
of those 'landlords, científicos, or bosses who oppose the present
plan' (Womack 1968: 402–3). The Zapatistas remained committed
to the revolutionary principles of the Plan of San Luis Potosí,
which called for the dismissal of all incumbent officials at both
local and federal levels, the free election and impartial appointment of new officials, and the judicial review of all disputed cases
involving rural real estate (Warman 1976: 97). The Zapatistas'
Plan of Ayala, however, went much further in its call for peasants
to reclaim lands immediately themselves and to defend them
by force of arms, without the need for approval by any higher
authority (97). The Plan of Ayala crystallized the radical spirit
at the heart of Zapatismo. In the words of Adolfo Gilly:

> Emiliano Zapata did not set out to destroy the capitalist system:
> his ideas sprang from the peasantry, not from a socialist program.

However, implementation of the Ayala Plan would have effectively smashed the living roots of capitalism. For it would have involved nationalization of all the property of the ruling classes. More important still — because actually applied by the peasantry — was the principle that the people themselves should decide, 'arms in hand'; that, instead of waiting for the revolution to triumph and enact the necessary leglislation, they would begin cultivating and defending the land. (Gilly 2005: 73)

The Zapatistas' Agrarian Law, issued on 26 October 1915, is as revolutionary as the Plan of Ayala. Most significantly, it signed into law principles regarding the return of land to individuals holding original title while enshrining the 'traditional and historic right which the pueblos, ranchos and communities of the Republic have of possessing and administering their fields of communal distribution ... and communal use ... in the form which they judge proper' (Womack 1968: 406). The Agrarian Law also codified the right of all Mexicans to possess enough land to cover their needs and those of their family, the rights of sharecroppers to own the land they work, and decreed inalienable the land ceded by the government to communities and individuals (407–9). The radical agrarian, deeply democratic nature of these twin decrees exemplified the principles for which the Zapatistas refused to lay down their arms. In the face of a compromised revolution co-opted by northern elites, the campesinos of Zapata's Liberating Army of the South refused to abandon their struggle for land, autonomy and justice.

In 1913, northern 'revolutionary' elites had become increasingly frustrated by Madero's apparent inability to put an end to radical agitation from below and pave the way for capitalist progress. To the north of the Rio Grande, some US officials were becoming increasingly concerned both about the revolutionary ferment still animating Mexico as well as Madero's failure to demobilize it (Warman 1976: 97). The coup that deposed Madero would be ani-

mated by both these interests and it began on 9 February 1913 as
elements of the federal army commanded by General Mondragón
revolted and freed generals Bernardo Reyes and Félix Díaz, who
had been imprisoned for attempting to engineer their own coups
against Madero (Gilly 2005: 91–2). Entrenching themselves in
the Ciudadela, the barracks and army depot of central Mexico
City, the coup forces were effectively surrounded by the Maderist
defenders, now under the command of General Victoriano Huerta
after Madero's chosen commander, General Villar, was wounded
in the initial assault (92). Despite his clear tactical advantage,
Huerta showed no interest in routing the coup forces or cutting
them off from supplies and after ten days of bloody and apparently
pointless conflict — known as the 'ten tragic days' — which left
many soldiers and civilians dead or wounded, a pact was signed
ending Madero's presidency and bringing the fighting to an end
(92). Signed in the US Embassy on 18 February 1913 by Huerta
for the besiegers and Díaz for the besieged, and with the clear
involvement of US Ambassador Henry Lane Wilson, the Embassy
Pact ended Madero's presidency, provisionally replaced him with
Huerta, called for the formation of a new cabinet, and allowed
coup plotter Díaz to run as a candidate in the next presidential
election (92). Francisco Madero and his vice president, José
María Pino Suárez, were arrested in the National Palace on 18
February, resigned their posts on 19 February, and were dead
two days later, murdered by their escort while being transferred
to Lecumberri Prison (92).

With Madero's assassination the revolutionary forces which
had overthrown Díaz now split into two distinct camps: the
reformists, also known as the Constitutionalists, led politically by
Venustiano Carranza and militarily by Alvaro Obregón, 'fought
for changes of a political nature within a legalistic framework';
and the radicals, led by Emiliano Zapata and Pancho Villa, who

demanded 'the immediate restructuring of the country' (Warman
1976: 98). Carranza was a wealthy landowner who had also been
a senator under Porfirio Díaz (Gilly 2005: 96). In the immediate aftermath of Huerta's coup against Madero, Carranza had
repudiated Huerta's authority and called for the defeat of his
'usurper government'(96). According to his Guadalupe Plan,
as commander-in-chief of the Constitutionalist forces, Carranza
would also assume executive power on an interim basis while
elections were called once Mexico City had been taken from
Huerta (96). On the back of the military acumen of Alvaro
Obregón and Pancho Villa, Huerta's forces were defeated and
Huerta himself handed over authority to an interim president,
Francisco Carbajal, on 15 July 1914 (121). At the time of Huerta's
defeat, four revolutionary armies occupied the national political and military landscape in Mexico: Emiliano Zapata and the
Liberating Army of the South; Pancho Villa and his Northern
Division, moving ever closer to an alliance with the Zapatistas and
towards a break with Carranza; Venustiano Carranza, supported
by Pablo González and his Northeast Army; and Alvaro Obregón
with his Northwest Army occupying Mexico City (124–5). Villa
and Zapata represented the radical left tendencies in the revolution, Carranza the right, and Obregón the centre (124–5). While
Obregón sought a negotiated settlement with the Villistas, Carranza's policy was one aimed at isolating and bloodily repressing
the Zapatistas and the Villistas and their much more radical
political programmes (125). Ultimately, it was the Obregón and
Carranza–González forces that occupied Mexico City, established
a provisional government, and drove a political and geographical
wedge between the Villistas and Zapatistas (125). The stage was
thus set for a head-on confrontation between the bourgeois and
radical trajectories within the Mexican Revolution.

As a way of heading off armed confrontation between the
forces of Carranza, Villa and Zapata, a convention of military
leaders was called, to open on 10 October 1914 on 'neutral ground'
in the town of Aguascalientes (Gilly 2005: 138). The Convention
was a site occupied by many different political ambitions. While
some sought to ward off armed conflict between the different
revolutionary forces, others saw the Convention as a place from
which to begin to legislate the aspirations of the revolution, and
still others saw in it an opportunity to do away with political
and military adversaries and consolidate their own power (140).
Ultimately, the Aguascalientes Convention facilitated what Carranza feared most, namely the political intersection of the Villistas
and Zapatistas, allowing the radical tendency of the revolution to
win control of the Convention government (141). Adopting the
Zapatistas' Plan of Ayala, the Convention also issued a 'minimum
programme' for the revolution, including: withdrawal of US forces
from Mexican territory; return of communal lands to villages; the
destruction of large landholdings and the return of land to the
people who work it; the nationalization of property belonging to
enemies of the revolution; and freedom of association and the
right of workers to strike (143). The Convention also decreed
that Carranza cede executive power and Villa step down as commander of the Northern Division while issuing no judgement as
a result of a lack of jurisdiction on Zapata because the Zapatistas
had not sent an official voting delegation (141). When Carranza
refused to abdicate his position, the Convention government
declared him a rebel and appointed Villa operational commander
of the two Convention armies — what amounted to the Northern
Division he already commanded (142). Seeing his opportunity to
consolidate his own vision and power through the Convention
gone, Obregón joined Carranza against Villa and Zapata (142).

What had begun as a political conflict had now formally escalated into a military one as well.

The Villistas and Zapatistas had claimed control of the Aguas-calientes Convention government and, in December 1914, their armies occupied Mexico City. In the words of Adolfo Gilly:

> The occupation of Mexico City by the peasant armies is one of the finest episodes of the entire revolution — an early, impetuous yet orderly show of strength that has left its mark on the country; one of the foundations that, unshaken by setbacks, treachery, and conflict, uphold the pride and self-respect of the Mexican peasantry. (2000: 149)

In spite of the euphoria of the moment, one representing the pinnacle of peasant struggle in the Mexican Revolution, stress fractures emerged immediately in the Convention government. The Villistas and Zapatistas had no interest in seizing power, they did not want to take command of the state, but because of this they ended up merely occupying it for the 'petit-bourgeois' politicians of the Convention government (Gilly 2000: 148). While the trajectory represented by the forces of Villa and Zapata was the most radical, most dispossessed, and most significant with respect to the revolution, this did not change the fact that neither Villa nor Zapata had initiated their insurrectionary actions in pursuit of power. In the words of Arturo Warman, the failure of Villa and Zapata to consolidate revolutionary power was:

> the result, not — as it is frequently presented — of the fear of power ... but of their congruence with a revolution that was being made from below and that still had not triumphed. The capture of the State, ever the enemy of the peasants, was not the Zapatistas' revolutionary objective; it was the consequence of a revolution at the base, in the free and sovereign villages. (1976, 100–101)

Warman's assessment of the failure of the Villa–Zapata forces to consolidate a revolutionary regime is profoundly significant and speaks to the way in which contemporary Zapatista rebels would situate and articulate their own struggle eight decades later. However, in the case of Villa and Zapata, by leaving the apparatus of the state to bureaucrats and the power structure of national government to compromised politicians, they remained true to the spirit animating their revolution while setting the stage for their own defeat. Rather than a failure to seize the state or power, the Zapatistas and Villistas failed to recognize that leaving a corrupt structure to operate in the background as revolutionary change was sought on the battlefield would result in the ultimate failure of the radical trajectory of the Mexican Revolution. While the Convention government failed to legislate the radical revolutionary spirit that had borne Villa and Zapata's armies to apparent victory in 1914, the Villistas and Zapatistas themselves failed to press home the tactical advantage they had over the Constitutionalists in the aftermath of the Aguascalientes Convention (see Gilly 2005: 162–73). Regular conflict between members of the revolutionary forces and government officials and bureaucrats — conflicts as much ideological as practical — only exacerbated the existing tension between these actors. This was the ideal situation for the forces of Obregón and Carranza; indeed, as time passed, the future for the Constitutionalist camp appeared considerably brighter than that of the radicals. In 1915, under the inspired command of Obregón, Constitutionalist forces delivered two severe military defeats to the Villistas (Warman 1976: 99). To make matters worse for the radical trajectory of the Mexican Revolution, in 1915 Carranza received diplomatic recognition of his government from the United States, effectively consolidating a Constitutionalist post-revolutionary government (99).

Despite the radicals' failure to form a revolutionary regime on a national level, the Zapatistas realized their agrarian revolution in Morelos in 1915. Land distribution, village autonomy, nationalization of production, and community-based consensus decision-making processes were all realized in Zapatista territory (Warman 1976: 102). Ultimately, however, the weight of Carranza's federal army and the repression brought to bear against the populace of Morelos, the inclusion of elements of agrarian reform in Article 27 of the new Constitution of 1917, and the isolation and deprivation faced by the Zapatistas took their toll (127–32). The final blow to this grassroots revolution would be delivered on 10 April 1919. Posing as a defector from the federal army, officer Jesús Guajardo lured Emiliano Zapata into an ambush with a promise of guns and ammunition (Vodovnik 2004: 34). Riding into Chinameca hacienda at the end of the Cuautla Valley, Morelos, Zapata was shot dead by federal troops as he passed through the archway (Vodovnik 2004: 34; Weinberg 2000: 56). Zapata's corpse was publicly displayed for two days in Cuautla with tens of thousands of campesinos coming to pay their last respects to the fallen revolutionary (Weinberg 2000: 56). Despite the public evidence of his death, rumours of Zapata's survival and continuing revolution abounded and indeed Zapata's generals continued the fight after his assassination (56). Ultimately, however, Zapata's assassination signalled the end of the radical trajectory of the Mexican Revolution and the beginning of a new post-revolutionary Mexico whose contours would largely be shaped by those whom Zapata had fought so dedicatedly against.

'Institutionalizing' a revolution

While Carranza's post-revolutionary regime was beginning to consolidate itself significant challenges lay ahead for elites attempting to craft a post-revolutionary state while still confronted by masses of radicalized peasants and workers. Not the least of these challenges would be the writing of a revolutionary history capable of tying the victorious post-revolutionary elites and their fragile state to the very revolutionary struggle they had worked so hard to crush.

In the years following the assassination of Emiliano Zapata, the post-revolutionary elite would be forced to confront mobilized masses both in the cities and in the countryside. In order to move forward with building a modern, capitalist nation-state, Mexico's post-revolutionary elite had to find ways of demobilizing these radicalized groups. While the strategies employed ranged from co-optation to outright repression, this process of demobilization and deradicalization could never be completely successful for the very reason that rural rebellion actually served as one of 'the modes of confirmation and existence' of the Mexican state community (Gilly 1998: 268). Rural rebellion was not only fundamental in giving birth to the post-revolutionary Mexican state, it was also fundamental in constructing the relationship between 'those who govern and those who are governed' (268). The only way that radicalized rural populations could be rearticulated as citizens of, rather than antagonists to, the newly emerging post-revolutionary Mexican state was by finding a way to bind them to the new regime.

Concretely, this binding occurred through the new Constitution of 1917 where peasants were included as significant social actors 'with status and specific rights as peasants, not simply as citizens' (Gilly 1998: 268). This status included peasants' expectation of protection by the state in exchange for their obedience to the ruling elite (268). Attempts to integrate the peasantry into the post-revolutionary architecture of power in Mexico began most effectively through the mechanism of land distribution. But radicalized peasants had been reclaiming land autonomously throughout the Revolution, so for land distribution to become a mechanism by which the peasantry could be de-radicalized and

integrated into the state it had to be made into a government
monopoly (Warman 1976: 141). Article 27 of the 1917 Constitution established the legal mechanism for the realization of this
monopoly by codifying the promise to peasants that by obeying
the state one might eventually win title to the land upon which
life depended. This is perhaps one of the most powerful legacies
of Mexican revolutionary history. Post-revolutionary elites sought
to consolidate their power, on the one hand, by laying claim
to a revolutionary legacy they had actively sought to subvert
and, on the other, by incorporating powerful groups within the
new power structure through new legalistic and nationalistic
mechanisms. The relationships and mutual obligations emerging from this new architecture of power would have profound
consequences for the state and for radical mobilization in Mexico
for years to come.

While 'peasants' entered into the post-revolutionary Mexican
state in explicit ways, indigenous peoples did not. In a trajectory established with the Spanish invasion of Mesoamerica, and
repeated throughout the Americas albeit in different forms, the
post-revolutionary Mexican state's official position with respect
to indigenous peoples was one aimed at their disappearance.
Embodied by the ideology of *indigenismo*, which involved 'the
assimilation and absorption of the indigenous in the Mexican, and
the "citizenization" of Indians through public education, state
protection, and economic development', the post-revolutionary
Mexican state sought to valorize an imagined and glorious
indigenous past while consigning actually existing indigenous
peoples to oblivion in the present (Gilly 1998: 278). Modernize
and disappear, or simply disappear, was the choice presented
to indigenous populations in Mexico after the Revolution. As is
true throughout the Americas, it was not a choice to which they
would resign themselves.

While elites in central Mexico were seeking to build a new post-revolutionary order commensurate with their national-ist dreams of modernization and capital accumulation, events were unfolding differently in the far south-east of the nation. Chiapas, future home of the Zapatista Army of National Lib-eration, had remained quiescent during the Revolution with its political landscape marked primarily by regional and largely inter-elite struggles for power and the control of indigenous labour (Benjamin 1996). Mirroring to a remarkable degree the elite struggles in central Mexico over who would enjoy the spoils of the Revolution, none of these struggles involved any degree of popular involvement, as tight systems of social and economic control as well as ethnic, geographical, and linguistic divisions and the absence of progressive leadership maintained an enforced passivity among the oppressed and exploited indig-enous population of the state (96). While the Revolution did not reach Chiapas, national and regional political crises associated with it created fractures in the 'paternalistic, repressive control of the landed elite over peasant villages and landless workers' (96). The weakening of this architecture of power facilitated popular politicization while opening up space for mobilization through vehicles such as political parties, agrarian communities and labour unions (96). A fuse of popular unrest had been lit in Chiapas, the truly explosive results of which would be seen in the decades to come.

As political organizing began to exploit the cracks in the power structure in Chiapas, at the national level the post-revolutionary order was about to be reformulated. Lázaro Cárdenas, a Constitu-tionalist general who had fought Villa's forces, occupied oilfields in Tampico, and served as governor of the state of Michoacan, was elected president in 1934 and immediately sought to fashion a post-revolutionary pact capable of reforging the Mexican nation

(Weinberg 2000: 57). Cárdenas was considerably to the left of
other post-revolutionary elites and it was under his regime that
land reform, the nationalization of key resources, and the incor-
poration of popular struggles into the apparatus of the state and
the ruling party occurred (57). Indeed, Cárdenas is remembered
as the president who created the 'corporatist' post-revolutionary
Mexican state that would endure for nearly six decades. Real-
izing that the party that emerged from the Revolution would not
survive if it did not consolidate its power by institutionalizing
its ties to the people, Cárdenas accomplished this by creating
national-level worker and peasant confederations that would
give these constituencies a 'seat at the table' while simultaneously working to channel dissent from below into acceptable
and manageable channels (Rus et al. 2003: 8). In combination
with the nationalization of the oil industry and the railroads,
land distribution and development initiatives, Cárdenas brought
stability to the post-revolutionary regime.

Seeing initiatives such as Cárdenas's simply as cynical attempts
at co-optation would be fundamentally to misunderstand the significance of these acts with respect to how the Mexican national
community was being constructed. As Gilly notes,

> the nationalization of oil and the (partial) redistribution of land
> came to be, rather like the living myth of the Mexican revolution,
> essential components of the form in which the national community
> imagined itself and of the ideology comprising Mexican nationalism.
> (1998: 271)

Through the appropriation of such figures as Emiliano Zapata
and Pancho Villa, the uneven and elite-controlled redistribution
of land, the formation of 'official' organs of 'sectoral' representation, and the consolidation of a paternalistic, corporatist state,
the post-revolutionary Mexican elite effectively foreclosed on
the possibility of radical and popular revolutionary action 'from

below'. The mythology of the Revolution became a powerful ideological weapon in this arsenal.

The situation was not very much different in Chiapas. What initially appeared to be powerful confederations of workers and peasants instead incorporated these groups into 'the party of the state' while the 'flawed but extensive advance of agrarian reform' led to the virtual immobilization of potentially revolutionary groups (Benjamin 1996: 210). Land reform served to fragment a broader indigenous movement as the state monopoly on land reform created communities closely tied to the state. Through the 1980s and early 1990s, these communities existed in a relationship of dependency with the state concretized through credit, material assistance and the amplification of their original land grants (210). In Chiapas, the government successfully subverted attempts to organize peasants and workers independently, imposing a co-opted model of 'official' and 'institutionalized' representation which served primarily as a source of legitimacy and support for the elite interests of large landowners, plantation owners and politicians.

As the post-revolutionary Mexican state consolidated itself, the grassroots capacity for dissent was channelled in very specific ways. As in any corporatist arrangement, channels for legal organization and expression of demands operated in post-revolutionary Mexico to reinforce the division between sectors, thus making them easier to control (Carr 1992: 81). Ideologically, by laying claim to the revolutionary pedigree of leaders like Hidalgo, Morelos, Zapata and Villa, the political elite could subvert dissent through appeals to revolutionary nationalist pride. When independent labour organizations did emerge between 1947 and 1949, the government response was not to acknowledge the validity of these organizations but to replace independent and combative leaders with *charros* (corrupt labour bosses) (188).

When confronted by radicalized teacher, railway, telephone, and metal trades workers' struggles in the 1950s, the government did not hesitate to respond with force, revealing the darker side of corporatism (201–7). Through a combination of 'revolutionary' ideological coercion, corporatist political architecture, cunning mechanisms of co-optation like land distribution, and the naked use of brutal force, Mexican post-revolutionary elites successfully and ruthlessly managed dissent. By the 1960s, however, fractures would begin to emerge in this edifice of co-optation and control, paving the way for the emergence of new radical actors in Mexico.

Fractures

Through the 1950s and the 1960s Chiapas found itself in the midst of an economic boom. Cattle ranching and the exportation of crops such as coffee, cacao, sugar cane and cotton led the way and large landowners benefited greatly from this boom period (Benjamin 1996: 223–6). For *ejidatarios* — those living and working on communally held land redistributed by the state — the situation was nowhere near as beneficial. While land had been redistributed to constitute these *ejidos*, many of the parcels were too small to support a single family, forcing *ejidatarios* to sell their labour to neighbouring estates or to work as migrant workers. Compounding this was the environmental degradation resulting from the high population density on the *ejidos* themselves. While constituting nearly half of all landowners, smallholders occupied less than 1 per cent of the land. Only 2.4 per cent of the population, large landowners possessing more than 1,000 hectares, owned nearly 60 per cent of the land (226). In the short term, the social peace was maintained largely through the use of 'safety valves' like land redistribution and socio-economic programmes organized by the National Indigenist Institute (228). These initiatives, however, could not stem the emergence of a 'grassroots, widespread, and increasingly organized agrarian struggle' in Chiapas in the 1970s (229). As the national context was marked by greater agitation, dissent and militancy, and with the entrenched Partido Revolucionario Institucional (PRI, Institutional Revolutionary Party) regime seemingly unable to suppress these manifestations of unrest, the rural poor of Chiapas were moving toward direct confrontation with the architectures and heirs of power that had dominated them for so long.

Mexico in the 1960s saw the emergence of new militant leftist actors on its political stage, including students, Christian activists, mass organizations and guerrilla groups. Inspired by Maoism, Trotskyism and the Cuban Revolution, newly radicalized students situated their demands broadly within the context of democracy in Mexico, defying the PRI's narrowly sectoral corporatism (Carr 1992: 229-30). In the wake of Vatican II, the 1968 Medellín conference, and liberation theology, many Protestant and Catholic activists in Mexico were also radicalized. Faced with considerable hostility from Church authorities, many lay Catholic activists broke completely with church orthodoxy and turned towards worker and peasant movements (231). In addition to this, the elements of the left in Mexico found themselves galvanized by the success of the Cuban Revolution. The Cuban example was particularly significant in this regard in three distinct ways: first, it challenged conventional stagist models of revolution espoused by established — and largely tamed — left actors such as the Mexican Communist Party; second, it inspired a new commitment to the route of armed struggle in Mexico, most notably in the states of Chihuahua and Guerrero; third, it put anti-imperialism and 'proletarian internationalism' back on the agenda, resulting in the formation of the National Liberation Movement (MLN) in

1961 (232-3). Representing a broad spectrum of interests from socialists to liberals, the MLN concerned itself primarily with defending the Cuban Revolution, reviving agrarian reform, struggling to free political prisoners, and establishing and defending economic and national independence (233). In this context, new radical actors would emerge to challenge the PRI's hegemony and to advance visions of other possible socio-political and economic orders.

By the 1970s, mass popular movements made up of neighbourhood residents, students, teachers and poor peasants began to emerge (Carr 1992: 235). In addition to struggling for a variety of particular goals, these popular movements took part in a more general struggle to constitute 'the people' as political actors in their own right, outside of the institutionalized channels and spaces (Foweraker 1990: 5). These new popular fronts were oriented toward shorter-term objectives and local movements rather than the longer-term, strategic goals of conventional political actors like parties and unions (Carr 1992: 236). Instead of playing a game of power politics aimed at capturing state power, these new movements sought to expand the autonomy of the people who constituted them. Emphasizing autonomy, direct democracy and social justice, these new popular movements represented an explicit challenge to the poverty of conventional politics and their superficial ideological revolutionary trappings.

Of all the movements involved in cracking the powerful edifice of the 'institutionalized revolution' in Mexico, none was more significant than the 1968 student movement. Set in motion by a series of violent, but initially politically insignificant, clashes between students and police in July 1968, the movement escalated to become an explicit challenge to the PRI and the anti-democratic nature of Mexican society (Carr 1992: 258-9). The structure of the student mobilization was as fluid as its ideological make-up.

Coordinated by the National Strike Council but made up of largely independent 'struggle committees' with no permanent or centralized leadership, the movement was informed by political ideologies ranging from 'revolutionary nationalism and internationalism ... [to] liberal democratic, Marxist, anarchist, and Maoist doctrines' (260–64). Resisting all forms of co-optation and division, the student mobilization posed a powerful and unavoidable challenge to the empty corporatism of the post-revolutionary Mexican state and, in so doing, earned its wrath. On 2 October 1968, after occupying the campuses of dissident universities, the army surrounded a large gathering of students and citizens at the Plaza of the Three Cultures in Mexico City and opened fire (263). Massive waves of arrests and violent repression followed the massacre and the movement was crushed. Smashed, too, was the illusion that the political architecture of Mexico was anything less than a vehicle for the interests and ambitions of the ruling elite. The consequences of the government's brutal repression of the student movement would be far-reaching indeed.

The Tlatelolco massacre convinced many Mexicans that to struggle against the PRI elites guiding the 'institutionalized revolution' was an exercise in futility — or worse. But for others, it was the clearest possible demonstration of the necessity of armed struggle. Between 1968 and 1973, an urban guerrilla struggle emerged in Mexico testifying to a new radical trajectory of resistance, a trajectory that was ultimately bloodily and ruthlessly crushed by the Mexican military (Carr 1992: 267). While these diverse struggles did not unseat the PRI, they did reveal the illegitimate nature of the corporatist 'revolutionary' state. Shattered was the PRI's fiction that its corporate political machinery effectively represented the demands of large sectors of the population. Gone, too, was any shred of democratic pretention on the part of the party-state. Perhaps most significant of all, the

government's draconian response to popular mobilization eroded
the last vestiges of the revolutionary heritage post-revolutionary
elites had draped themselves in for so long. Subordinated and
marginalized populations in Mexico were now heading towards
direct conflict with the heirs of power, who, without the legacy
of the Revolution to cling to, now appeared to many Mexicans
as little more than usurpers and dictators.

Desperate to recover some shred of legitimacy for their shaken
'institutional revolution', PRI governments through the 1970s
and early 1980s sought to open spaces for participation and
engagement within existing corporatist structures (Carr 1992:
273–80). Compounding the political crisis generated by the
PRI regime's bankrupt democratic pretensions was the financial crisis of 1976–77. Inflation, ballooning foreign debt, high
interest rates, and a balance-of-payments deficit provoked the
direct intervention of the International Monetary Fund and the
implementation of a drastic austerity program, creating a radically new economic environment within which the PRI would
have to operate (279). Nothing would challenge the corporatist
party-state of the PRI and its revolutionary mythology as seriously as the reshaped political-economic terrain imposed by
this financial restructuring. In 1982, in the wake of this massive
financial restructuring, the collapse of oil prices led to a full-
blown crisis. Corporatism had always depended on capital to
grease the wheels of its political machinery. In a new economic
environment marked by austerity, 'the PRI — a party whose
existence was tied to state corporatism — itself undertook to
dismantle that corporatism and remake itself in the 1980s as the
party of structural adjustment and neoliberal economics' (Rus et
al. 2003: 11). As is true the world over, the consequences of this
neoliberal restructuring were felt immediately by workers and
peasants in the form of drastically decreased expenditures on

everything from health care and education to guaranteed agricultural prices and subsidies for basic foodstuffs. Severe as these impacts were for workers and peasants, they would prove even more devastating for the PRI itself — 'Without money to grease the wheels, the patron–client system simply ceased to function' (11). Economic liberalization without political democratization would prove to be far too much for the PRI's hollowed-out mythology of 'institutionalized revolution' to sustain.

As neoliberal economics facilitated the collapse of the corporatist post-revolutionary political system in Mexico while eroding the standard of living for broad swathes of the population, several broad popular fronts and organizations emerged marking a new wave of resistance and alternative-building in Mexico. The emergence of these new fronts represented a significant shift in the focus of organizing and resistance from the workplace to the spaces and places where people were living their lives — the neighbourhood, the street, the school (Carr 1992: 281). These new sites of struggle revolved around issues such as access to land, housing and urban services like potable water, roads and electricity (281). On 19 September 1985 a huge earthquake devastated Mexico City; when the government and military utterly failed to provide rapid response or relief, the civilian population mobilized in a dedicated and well-coordinated rescue and rebuilding effort (Cockcroft 1998: 280). Political crisis compounded by economic crisis, magnified by the failure to provide basic services to the civilian population, left many Mexicans wondering what the PRI offered in return for their obedience. Finally, in 1988, Cuauhtémoc Cárdenas, son of the populist president of the 1930s, electorally defeated the PRI candidate Carlos Salinas de Gortari only to have the presidency stolen from him through widespread 'computer failure' on election night (300). The PRI retained power but its legitimacy had been extensively undermined.

The significance of these multiple crises for the PRI should not be understated. The PRI's power radiated not only from its material, institutional and coercive capacities but from its appropriation and deployment of a revolutionary heritage which it at least needed to appear to nurture and defend. The appropriation of this revolutionary history did not simply function to allow post-revolutionary elites to legitimate their power and to present their interests as identical to the interests of the Mexican people and the nation. This revolutionary heritage also articulated the bases and terms upon which the rulers and the ruled were mutually beholden to one another as a consequence of the Revolution itself. As Mexican scholar Adolfo Gilly asserts, 'If that [social] pact originating in the armed revolution has now been broken, even if only symbolically, the right to take up arms is once again ours' (1998: 269). Thus, in the 1980s, out of the economic and political fractures splitting the PRI's hegemony, a political opening had been created within which alternative forms of organization and mobilization could emerge. In effect, the legacy and possibility of rebellion and revolution were increasingly being reclaimed by popular movements. It is within this context that in the far south-east of Mexico, the Zapatista Army of National Liberation began to take shape.

The seeds of rebellion in Chiapas

The rural poor of Chiapas had learned the bitter truth of 'institutional organizing' and by the 1970s were increasingly turning to independent labour, agrarian and community organization. The Zapatista rebellion of 1994 is a direct continuation of this type of organizing as well as an outgrowth of the revolutionary trajectories described throughout this chapter. Faced with a past and present marked by incredible violence, exploitation, racism, co-optation and contempt, and witnessing the dissolution of the post-revolutionary social pact, organizing among the indigenous peasants of Chiapas took on an increasingly militant and independent character. Perhaps even more significant, however, is the spirit which came to animate organization, militancy and rebellion in Chiapas. In the words of Adolfo Gilly:

> rebellions present themselves as secular and successive collective acts, material and symbolic, at times very diverse in the immediate motivations apparent to their participants, but whose ultimate content could be found in the will of these communities to persist. The participants resist and rise up in order to persist, because they can persist only by resisting the movement of a world that dissolves and negates their Being. (1998: 263–4)

As multiplying crises undermined the co-optative mechanisms of the PRI's corporatist party–state, and the demands of neoliberal economic restructuring and an eroded revolutionary legitimacy made its repressive machinery all the more apparent, indigenous communities in Chiapas prepared to defend themselves forcefully in the face of a world threatening to dissolve and negate their being.

The First Indian Congress took place in Chiapas in 1974 and was a major impetus for indigenous organizing in the state. Sponsored by Bishop Samuel Ruiz, the congress brought together Tzotzil, Tzeltal, Tojolabal and Chol leaders representing more than 300 communities (Benjamin 1996: 235). Emerging from this congress was a well-organized indigenous movement assisted not only by clergy and church workers but also by radical political activists from urban centres who had fled police and army repression or decided that the countryside would be a more fruitful venue for radical political organizing (235). During this time period, numerous political parties and organizations also began organizing in Chiapas (Hernández Navarro 1994: 7).

At the same time, unions of peasants and agricultural workers sprang up throughout the state (Benjamin 1996: 235–6). In the face of extensive attempts at repression and co-optation, these independent mobilizations would lay the groundwork for new and militant forms of popular contestation of government abuses and elite exploitation.

In the early 1980s, cadres from an urban guerrilla organization entered Chiapas to add the last element necessary to give rise to the Zapatista Army of National Liberation. Formed in the north of Mexico in 1969 by survivors of earlier guerrilla initiatives, the Forces of National Liberation (Fuerzas de Liberación Nacional, FLN) had sent operatives into the highlands of Chiapas in order to initiate a new front of armed struggle in preparation for the anticipated protracted politico-military national struggle necessary to install a socialist system (Womack 1999: 36). Indeed, Subcomandante Insurgente Marcos, military leader and spokesperson of the Zapatista Army of National Liberation, would recount years later that the EZLN was born on 17 November 1983 in a meeting attended by three indigenous people and three mestizos (Harvey 1998: 164; see also Muñoz Ramírez 2008). In 1984, along with the first group of guerrillas, Marcos went to live in the Lacandón Jungle's harsh mountainous terrain and it is there that the urban and Marxist core of the EZLN came face to face with the indigenous culture and heritage of Chiapas, a confrontation which would force the former to reconfigure and subordinate itself to the latter (Harvey 1998: 165–6). The 'defeat' of Marxist dogma by the cultural and historical force of indigenous reality in Chiapas allowed the EZLN to expand and to begin recruiting new members from communities.

Attempts were made in the 1980s by government to respond to the increasingly militant and mobilized rural poor in Chiapas. Temporarily exchanging the stick for the carrot, the state sought to ameliorate the symptoms of systemic and entrenched inequality in Chiapas through initiatives such as the World Bank-sponsored $300 million 'Plan Chiapas' and the Program of Agrarian Rehabilitation, which operated by compensating estate and plantation owners for lands invaded by peasants (Harvey 1998: 247). However, even as these initiatives were introduced in an effort to pacify the state, the De la Madrid federal government also issued 2,932 certificates of agricultural ineffectability and 4,714 certificates of ranching ineffectability, protecting 'productive', and elite-owned, land from reform (248). Land invasions by independent campesino organizations continued and were met by violent expulsions and repression (249).

With tensions in Chiapas already running high, social unrest and grassroots militancy were further amplified by three key events at both national and international levels: first, the international price of coffee collapsed; second, credit available from the state for small producers contracted profoundly; third, price supports for corn growers were eliminated, coupled with an obligation for them to compete against agribusiness on the international market (Gilly 1998: 290). In true neoliberal form, the post-revolutionary corporatist state occupied by the PRI was systematically divesting itself of even the most modest claims to being the guarantor of social justice. In so doing, the PRI regime signalled to the Mexican nation that the pact of social peace based on the recognition of mutual obligation between the rulers and the ruled established after the Mexican Revolution was effectively over. By themselves, this set of initiatives may have provoked indigenous communities in Chiapas to take up arms against state and national elites who had clearly abandoned them to the whims of the 'free market'. As it unfolded, however, there still remained several key developments before armed rebellion moved from threat to reality.

The first of these key events was the audacious electoral fraud that robbed Cuauhtémoc Cárdenas of his presidential victory in 1988. With polls showing Cárdenas clearly in the lead, election computers suffered a massive 'breakdown', and when they came back up Cárdenas had lost to PRI candidate Carlos Salinas de Gortari (Gilly 1998: 291). This fraud was regarded widely as a blatant violation of the post-revolutionary social pact. The second key event was the appointment of Patrocinio González Garrido to the post of secretary of the interior in 1992. As governor of Chiapas since 1989, González Garrido cultivated a reputation for himself as a cunning and brutal oppressor of popular movements as well as being an instrumental actor in building ties between the Chiapan oligarchy and the increasingly neoliberal elite outside of Chiapas — particularly those in the Salinas government (292). González Garrido's promotion to secretary of the interior would achieve three very different outcomes simultaneously. First, his promotion indicated the abandonment of the nationalist sector on the part of the state while leaving the Salinas government without the skills and experience of the previous secretary of the interior who was well-versed in matters of internal security and effectively combining repression with negotiation (292). Second, it cemented the ties between the Chiapan oligarchy and the federal government, leaving González Garrido both to prepare Mexico's internal affairs for the implementation of NAFTA and for the upcoming federal election (292). Third, González Garrido's promotion removed from Chiapas a man who had been particularly effective at infiltrating, containing, repressing and destroying popular movements (292). Ironically, as state socialism was collapsing in Eastern Europe and neoliberal elites were crowing about the 'end of history', conditions in Chiapas were actually pushing some communities towards an armed rebellion that would shake the foundations of the new world order.

Enough!

Soon after ascending to the presidency, Carlos Salinas (1988–94) attempted to rework the fatally damaged post-revolutionary social pact into a neoliberal model. No longer capable of managing a corporatist structure, the Salinas government sought to reconfigure a political system based on patron–client relations into one based on citizen–state relationships (Rus et al. 2003: 11). The Salinas government also established the National Solidarity Program 'for small projects of community development and improvement' and while no state received more money from it than Chiapas, it was once again a situation of too little too late as no single programme could have hoped to make a dent in the massive poverty and inequality endemic to the state (Harvey 1998: 251). The match was put to the fuse of rebellion in 1992 when the Salinas government reformed Article 27 of the Constitution in order to lay the foundation for the implementation of NAFTA. This reform removed the rights of campesinos to petition for land redistribution and made *ejido* land open to privatization in order to encourage capitalist investment in agriculture. On the ground in Chiapas, it was the final piece setting the stage for a head-on confrontation between the state, large landowners and the peasantry.

In this context, a new grassroots peasant organization emerged in the highlands, eastern frontier and north of Chiapas. Calling itself the Alianza Nacional Campesina Independiente Emiliano Zapata (ANCIEZ, Emiliano Zapata Independent National Peasant Alliance), it was the first public face of the Zapatista Army of National Liberation (Harvey 1998 253; Womack 1999: 39). For some time, the case for armed rebellion had been advocated for by people working in the Lacandón Jungle and several communities in the highlands on the basis of 'the explosive combination of unresolved land claims, lack of social services, institutional atrophy, authoritarian political bosses, monstrous deformations in the justice system, and the general lack of democracy' (Hernández Navarro 1994: 8). On 12 October 1992, in commemoration of five hundred years of survival and resistance, thousands of indigenous people flooded the streets of the colonial city of San Cristóbal de las Casas and toppled the statue of the city's conquistador founder Diego de Mazariegos (Gilly 1998: 293-4; see also Hernández Navarro 1994). As would later become apparent, this demonstration was a trial run for the uprising on 1 January 1994.

On 1 January 1994, the Zapatista Army of National Liberation began its armed rebellion against the Mexican federal executive and elements of the state that supported and defended it by seizing several towns and hundreds of ranches in Chiapas. In 'The First Declaration of the Lacandón Jungle', the Zapatista declaration of war, the General Command of the EZLN states that 'we are a product of five hundred years of struggle', explicitly narrating a history of struggle not only of indigenous peoples against Spanish invaders, but of the people of Mexico against invasion, dictatorship, poverty, and repression (EZLN 2001a: 13). While asserting their goal to advance on the Mexican capital and depose the federal executive in order to allow 'the people liberated to elect, freely and democratically, their own administrative authorities', the Zapatistas also outline the central goals of their struggle: 'work, land, housing, food, health care, education, independence, freedom, democracy, justice, and peace' (14). Speaking to the demands of campesinos in the Mexican south-east today, as well as invoking the legacy of five centuries of struggle, the Zapatistas' declaration sought to legitimize the rebellion as an act of necessity in the face of a system seeking to impose oblivion upon those most peripheral to it.

At the time of the uprising, the Zapatistas' rebellion appeared almost anachronistic — a throwback to an earlier era of revolution ill suited to a world in which neoliberal capitalism appeared globally ascendant, the USA stood as its lone superpower, and dreams of state-sponsored socialism lay shattered among the rubble of the fallen Berlin Wall. In fact, as Marcos and other Zapatista leaders have asserted in interviews and communiqués published since the uprising, leading up to the uprising there was considerable divergence between the leadership of the EZLN and its base communities with respect to the potential for armed rebellion. This discrepancy speaks to the different ways in which the leadership of the EZLN and its base situated and conceived of their struggle. As Adolfo Gilly asserts:

> The channels through which communities, on one side, and the leadership of the EZLN (or for that matter any other left-wing organization), on the other, get their perceptions of the surrounding society are not the same; nor are the filters and the codes according to which they are interpreted. This difference, invisible to all in 'normal' times when the capital decision — insurrection — is not in play, comes to light at the moment of making that decision. For that reason, while some see in the 'disappearance of the Soviet Union' a negative factor, others who are distant from that interpretation of an upheaval, regarding which they are not concerned, measure by other methods — against the arc of their own lives — the maturation of conditions for rebellion. (1998: 303)

In place of geopolitical analysis, theoretical orthodoxy, or even a narrow pragmatism, indigenous communities in Chiapas measured the conditions, cost and possibility of rebellion 'against the arc of their own lives', a perspective that would deeply infuse Zapatismo as political praxis in the years following the uprising.

2

'Everything for everyone, nothing for ourselves'

ZAPATISMO AS POLITICAL PHILOSOPHY
AND POLITICAL PRACTICE

WHEN THE Zapatista Army of National Liberation exploded onto the political stage at national and international levels on 1 January 1994, the rebellion seemed to many to have come out of nowhere. Indeed, what the Mexican government and military did know about the existence of the EZLN had been very intentionally kept quiet due to Mexican elites' fear that public knowledge of the existence of a rebel group in Chiapas would derail the fast-tracked ratification of NAFTA by exposing Mexico as a risky trading partner and investment site. As a clandestine organization for its first ten years, the EZLN itself had made no public pronouncements in the lead-up to the uprising; nor had it established formal channels of communication or coordination with other dissident actors. Thus, the origins, organizing principles, ideology, and goals of the EZLN were a mystery to most Mexicans and to those observing from afar. This mystery would not remain in place for long, however, and as the 1 January uprising lifted the curtain on the rebel existence of the EZLN much more would become known not only about the concrete dimensions of the movement but about its novel and radical approach to envisioning and practising politics. In this chapter, I take up an examination of Zapatismo — the political philosophy and practice of the Zapatista movement — particularly as it relates to the Zapatistas as a rebel movement of global significance.

Fire and word

In the first hours of the rebellion, the EZLN made several public statements aimed at communicating key issues animating its uprising to Mexicans, statements that were picked up by activist networks and journalists and transmitted globally. These statements, and the political imagination they reflected, would be the first words spoken in what would become a very protracted conversation between the Zapatistas and those they identified broadly as 'civil society' both within and outside Mexico.

The Zapatistas' first public word, the Zapatista declaration of war, was addressed to the Mexican people in the form of 'The First Declaration of the Lacandón Jungle'. In addition to explaining the reasons and aims of the uprising it also speaks directly to the issue of what the Zapatistas hoped for in terms of Mexican society's response:

> To the People of Mexico,
> We, the men and women, full and free, are conscious that the war that we have declared is our last resort, but also a just one. The dictators are applying an undeclared genocidal war against our people for many years. Therefore we ask for your participation, your decision to support this plan that struggles for work, land, housing, food, health care, education, independence, freedom, democracy, justice and peace. We declare that we will not stop fighting until the basic demands of our people have been met by forming a government of our country that is free and democratic.
> JOIN THE INSURGENT FORCES OF THE ZAPATISTA NATIONAL LIB-ERATION ARMY. (EZLN 2001a: 15)

While the EZLN declared its intention to advance on Mexico City, overcome the federal army, depose the federal executive and allow for free and democratic elections, the shape of the Zapatistas' insurgency would ultimately bear little resemblance to the revolutionary agenda established in this initial Declaration. Furthermore, while Mexican civil society would indeed respond to the Zapatista uprising, it would not be in the way that the Zapatistas had originally called for. Beyond the national context, the Zapatista uprising would reverberate far beyond the borders of Mexico, entering into a complex and unanticipated transnational dialogue with many different dissident actors elsewhere.

One of the very first indications that the Zapatista Army of National Liberation was something other than the familiar Maoist or Guevarist insurgency inhabiting so much of Latin American history came on the very first day of the uprising. In an impromptu interview following the EZLN's liberation of San Cristóbal de las Casas, the old colonial capital of Chiapas, an insurgent calling himself Subcomandante Insurgente Marcos provided the following explanation for the uprising:

> what was needed was for someone to give a lesson in dignity, and this fell to the most ancient inhabitants of this country that is now called Mexico, but when they were here it did not have a name, that name. It fell to the lowest citizens of this country to raise their heads, with dignity. And this should be a lesson for all. We cannot let ourselves be treated this way, and we have to try and construct a better world, a world truly for everyone, and not only a few, as the current regime does. This is what we want. We do not want to monopolize the vanguard or say that we are the light, the only alternative, or stingily claim the qualification of revolutionary for one or another current. We say, look at what happened. That is what we had to do.
>
> We have dignity, patriotism and we are demonstrating it. You should do the same, within your ideology, within your means,

within your beliefs, and make your human condition count. (Sub-comandante Marcos 2002a: 211–12)

While some have claimed that the EZLN's indigenous charac-ter and the rhetoric of dignity, radical democracy and inclusivity were cunning political flourishes made by the Zapatista leadership to mobilize international support only after the rebellion began (see Meyer 2002; Oppenheimer 2002), Marcos's invocation of these elements as well as his explicit renunciation of revolution-ary vanguardism on the first day of the uprising point instead to the fundamental nature of these principles for the Zapatistas. Significantly, these principles speak to the very foundations of the EZLN and the cultural–political matrix out of which it emerged in the early 1980s.

While the Zapatista Army of National Liberation appeared publicly for the first time on 1 January 1994, when thousands of EZLN guerrillas seized several towns and hundreds of ranches in Chiapas, its origins lie a decade before this moment. From the moment of its public emergence, the EZLN appeared at once familiar within the pantheon of revolutionary struggle in Latin America and radically different from it. An examination of the socio-historical roots of Zapatismo offers compelling insight into why.

Rebel roots

For indigenous peoples throughout the Americas, the last five centuries have been characterized by exploitation, oppression, neglect, racism and outright genocide. The project of explora-tion, conquest and appropriation embarked upon by the imperial European powers in the fifteenth century shaped the geopolitical order as we know it today. At its core, this project was predi-cated upon the fundamental denial of the dignity, integrity and autonomy of entire peoples. For the indigenous Mayan population of Chiapas, as for indigenous peoples throughout the rest of the Americas, the broad contours of this story remained the same, with the specificity of context providing the details unique to each place. While the Zapatista rebellion needs to be understood within this centuries-long context, the conditions which gave birth to the EZLN originated only decades ago (Womack 1999: 13).

Many indigenous communities in Chiapas did not join the Zapatista movement, and understanding why some did while others did not sheds considerable light on Zapatismo as political philosophy and political practice. Beginning in the 1950s, villages in Chiapas's south-east region of Los Altos experienced a profound transformation from communities that were tightly knit to conflict-ridden, elite-dominated ones (Womack 1999: 13). State political leaders and elites from San Cristóbal made use of development programmes for Tzotzil and Tzeltal villages run by the National Indigenist Institute (INI) to extend their own influence and control over these communities. Binding indigenous communities to them through resources provided by the INI, state and local elites effectively undermined the traditional processes of law, custom, prestige and authority upon which the indigenous communities had relied for so long. By the 1970s, the indigenous communities surrounding San Cristóbal had bilingual teachers from the ruling Institutional Revolutionary Party as their municipal presidents. Tellingly, these presidents were described not in terms of Mayan tradition but rather as *caciques* — 'bosses' — a term drawn from Mexican national political culture (13). As these PRI bosses imposed political control and 'unity' within their jurisdictions, the communities of Los Altos were also changing demographically. As medical services improved, death rates declined, but birth rates did not and communities found themselves faced with the serious problem of an increasing population with limited available resources — including land (14). The 'unity' of the communities was thus at a critical breaking point.

While the indigenous communities surrounding San Cristóbal were only undergoing these radical changes in the 1950s, indigenous Chols, Tzotzils, Tzeltals and Tojolabals in the highlands' northern and eastern valleys and southern plains around the towns of Altamirano, Ocosingo and Las Margaritas were already living in new communities that were radically different (Womack 1999: 14). As discussed in the previous chapter, thanks to the Liberal Reform Laws and the modern project of capitalist development, indigenous communities had been 'freed' from the shackles of tradition to sell their labour on the open market. Of course, rather than the realization of a liberal utopia, this 'freedom' opened the door to new and expansive forms of exploitation. For generations, indigenous families had worked as indentured labour on coffee, sugar and cattle estates, and their allegiances were owed solely to their landlord. However, with the reform of the agrarian law following the Mexican Revolution — the concession made by post-revolutionary elites in order to demobilize the radicalized peasantry — these indigenous families found common cause with one another in order to try and achieve something they had previously thought impossible: to petition for and communally hold land to farm (14). Facing considerable — and often violent — resistance from political bosses and landowners, these indigenous communities were drawn together out of necessity in a manner that insisted on tight-knit communities of common concern and collective action and articulated new forms of indigenous action in Chiapas. People organized collectively to find, occupy and defend — politically and physically — grantable land. If the state granted the land to the new community as an *ejido*, communally held and worked farmland, it was then defended as the joint trust of its founders (15).

Unfortunately, since the state maintained a monopoly on land redistribution, the winning of these *ejidos* relied upon the favour of political elites, thus encouraging the rise of another generation of *caciques* who sought to maintain 'unity' and establish links to local and regional elites (Womack 1999: 15). As with the communities around San Cristóbal, here too population growth compounded political domination and soon there were too many people and not enough land (15). Throughout Los Altos, challenges to community unity, land and resource shortages, greedy and dominating bosses, and an exploding population were leading young and landless indigenous to migrate to the east into the canyons and then into the Lacandón jungle.

For political elites, migration to the Lacandón jungle offered a viable escape valve for the social unrest brewing in Los Altos. For the young indigenous migrants, the communities they formed in the Lacandón Jungle offered an opportunity to experiment with social and political organization. Left to themselves, faced with common concerns, and bereft of their traditional leaders and ranks of honour, these migrants chose to emphasize the importance of community and thus turned to the assembly where all people over the age of 16 would meet to reach consensus over all decisions which affected the community (Womack 1999: 18). Within this system of assemblies, it was not the authorities that were seen as ruling the community but the community that was seen as ruling the authorities (19). In the years to come, these new communities would become the base and backbone of the Zapatista movement and their assembly-based form of direct democracy would become one of the hallmarks of Zapatismo.

While the communities formed by Chol, Tojolobal, Tzeltal and Tzotzil migrants would become the Zapatista base, another vital element in the emergence of this movement would arrive out of the failed urban guerrilla struggles in Mexico. Indeed, contemporary Zapatismo originated out of the encounter between indigenous communities in the Lacandón jungle and highlands of Chiapas and the urban revolutionaries who arrived in the state in the early 1980s. The EZLN itself was born in a camp in Chiapas on 17 November 1983 with six insurgents — three mestizos and three indigenous — present (Muñoz Ramírez 2008: 21). While these urban revolutionaries — cadres from the Fuerzas de Liberación Nacional (Forces of National Liberation, FLN) — arrived in Chiapas to organize campesinos for a revolution, this encounter resulted not in the 'revolutionizing' of the indigenous communities but in the 'defeat' of Marxist dogma at the hands of these indigenous realities, a defeat that actually allowed for the emergence of the Zapatista struggle itself. While Subcomandante Marcos, who would become the Zapatistas' spokesperson and one of their chief military strategists, and the other guerrillas arrived via the city with their world-views shaped by the ideological discourse of Marxism, the indigenous communities they encountered grounded their existence in a very different understanding of the world.

As political scientist Neil Harvey describes, to the indigenous communities of Chiapas, the rugged, mountainous terrain where Marcos and the other guerrillas first lived upon their arrival was not merely a location well suited to concealing the nascent EZLN; more importantly it was 'a respected and feared place of stories, myths, and ghosts' (1998: 165). Marcos and the other urban revolutionaries began to realize that indigenous notions of time, history and reality were fundamentally different from what they had been taught to believe (165). As Harvey explains, for these urban guerrillas, '[l]earning the indigenous languages and understanding their own interpretations of their history and culture led to an appreciation of the political importance of patience' (166).

This lesson in patience would come to characterize Zapatismo for years to come.

Learning from the indigenous communities and ultimately subordinating their own preconceptions to the realities they encountered in Chiapas had a profound effect not only upon the mestizo (mixed heritage) Zapatistas; it also proved vital to the formation of the EZLN itself. 'Instead of arriving directly from the city or the university, the EZLN emerged out of *la montaña*, that magical world inhabited by the whole of Mayan history, by the spirits of ancestors, and by Zapata himself' (Harvey 1998: 166). While Marcos had come to teach politics and history to the indigenous of Chiapas, he quickly discovered that this revolutionary education, steeped in its own assumptions, made no sense to the communities. The emergent politics of this encounter — and what would ultimately become Zapatismo — required a new language, one that was born of the urban revolutionaries' critical reading of Mexican history and current economic and political context, combined with the communities' own histories of genocide, racism, suffering, and exclusion. This new political discourse would achieve its most powerful form once it was translated into the local Mayan languages (166). In the canyons and Lacandón Jungle of Chiapas, the Chol, Tzeltal, Tzotzil and Tojolabal Mayan migrants who had been practising communal decision-making in a directly democratic way through community assemblies found their political practice further radicalized in light of the emerging politics of Zapatismo.

In this setting, the community ruled while the authorities obeyed (Womack 1999: 19). This relationship exemplifies the key Zapatista democratic notion of 'commanding obeying', as all authority and legitimacy in this case reside in the community and in the assembly rather than in military strongmen or political bosses. As Harvey notes, 'the support base of the EZLN inverted the traditional leader–masses relationship and provided a distinctive model of popular and democratic organization' (Harvey 1998, 166–7). The radically democratic nature of Zapatismo is one of the key elements that drew others within and outside of Mexico to the Zapatista struggle following the rebellion.

It is significant to note that in calling themselves 'Zapatista', the insurgents of the EZLN and the civilian base that comprises the bulk of the movement have adopted the name of one of the greatest Mexican revolutionary heroes, but also one who was neither active nor particularly well known in Chiapas until relatively recently (Collier and Quaratiello 1999: 158). In fact, the source of the image and ideology of Zapata in Chiapas can be traced primarily to urban revolutionaries who went out into the countryside in the aftermath of 1968 to work with the rural population (Stephen 2002: 150). In the statutes of the Forces of National Liberation — the guerrilla organization whose cadres would help found the EZLN — written fourteen years before the Zapatista rebellion, the choice of Emiliano Zapata as the icon for the revolution is attributed to the fact that 'Emiliano Zapata is the hero who best symbolizes the traditions of revolutionary struggle of the Mexican people' (Forces of National Liberation 2003: 20). By invoking the man, his image and his legacy, the Zapatistas are currently engaged in a process not only of reaffirming the 'Mexicanness' of their movement, but also of asserting its legitimacy while laying claim to the authentic and uncompromised legacy of the Mexican Revolution.

Subcomandante Marcos has described the history of the EZLN up to the initiation of the Zapatista rebellion on 1 January 1994 as comprising seven stages (Muñoz Ramírez 2008: 20–28). The first stage, in the early 1980s, involved the selection of those urban guerrillas of the FLN who would become part of the EZLN. The second, Marcos refers to as 'implantation' — the actual

founding of the EZLN by six insurgents in a camp in Chiapas in
1983. The third stage, beginning in 1984, was characterized by
the insurgents of the EZLN learning to survive in the jungles of
Chiapas and to prepare themselves for armed insurrection, and
Marcos says it is during this period that he arrived in Chiapas.
The fourth stage of the EZLN's genesis prior to the January
1 uprising, taking place during the latter half of the decade,
involved the first contact between EZLN insurgents and members
of local indigenous communities as the Zapatistas began the
process of recruitment and expansion — a stage Marcos identifies
as particularly significant as he asserts that '[b]y then we had
been defeated by the indigenous communities, and as a product
of that defeat, the EZLN started to grow exponentially and to
become "very otherly"' (27-8). The fifth stage is described by
Marcos as one of 'explosive expansion' as political and economic
conditions in Chiapas drove more and more indigenous towards
the EZLN. The sixth stage involved the base communities of the
EZLN voting on and preparing for war.

By the time the sixth stage of the EZLN's development had
been reached, the Clandestine Revolutionary Indigenous Committee had been formally created and all ties to the EZLN's
urban guerrilla parent organization, the FLN, had been severed
(Womack 1999: 192). Perhaps most importantly, this sixth stage
marks the democratic decision taken by the communities themselves rather than the leadership — indigenous or not — of the
EZLN to rise up in arms, the last resort of a people pushed
to the brink by elite-driven political and economic projects
determined to negate their very being. The seventh and final
stage Marcos narrates is in the last days of 1993, immediately
before the uprising, as final combat preparations were made by
the EZLN for its war against oblivion (Muñoz Ramírez 2008:
29-31).

The stages Marcos describes here correspond to the recent history of the EZLN that I have sought to trace in this chapter, and they also reflect the significant local, regional and national developments I outlined in the previous chapter. The significance of these stages in terms of understanding Zapatismo as a rebel political philosophy and practice is that they highlight the dynamic and organic manner in which the Zapatista struggle emerged out of the social, cultural and political soil of Chiapas. Neither the EZLN nor Zapatismo is a product of a pure revolutionary trajectory. Indeed, this is what has made both of them so robust, powerful and significant both within the Mexican context and outside of it. Out of the confluence of urban guerrillas seeking favourable ground for revolutionary organizing, migrant indigenous communities practising a new kind of politics, and a socio-economic and political context marked by extreme violence, exploitation and repression, the EZLN and Zapatismo emerged as rebellious articulations of hope that the world could be remade into a more just, democratic and free place. While the arrival of cadres from the FLN in the jungles of Chiapas could be said to mark the beginning of this radical trajectory, it is in the defeat of the ideology of these urban guerrillas by the indigenous realities with which they came face to face in the far south-east of Mexico, where the true origins of Zapatismo are to be found. Taking the best lessons from the urban revolutionary legacy embodied by the cadres of the FLN, and perhaps most importantly by Subcomandante Marcos, the EZLN and Zapatismo only truly developed into powerful rebel challenges to the status quo once they were deeply grounded in the social fabric of the communities that came to constitute them. Tellingly, it was only once the ideological dogmatism of the urban revolutionaries had been defeated and replaced by an organic radical analysis born of the encounter of different worlds, the hierarchical links to the FLN severed, and the base communities established as the highest authority — formalized through the creation of the CCRI — that the EZLN and Zapatismo expanded exponentially. This novel approach to radical struggle and its promise of building a different world animate the national and transnational resonance of Zapatismo in the years following the uprising.

'A revolution to make a revolution possible': Zapatismo and women's rights

Since the beginning of the Zapatista uprising, much has been made of the fact that the EZLN has a significant number of women among its ranks. Women make up approximately 45 per cent of the Zapatista insurgents today, voluntarily renouncing having a family in order to participate in the armed struggle (Subcomandante Marcos 2008: 21). The international media have been particularly interested in this aspect of the Zapatistas struggle:

> mainstream media immediately latched on to the curious fact that many of the Zapatista soldiers in uniform who participated in the capture of various towns and communication centers in January 1994 were women ... which has often been reflected in the media through the 'shocking' image of young Maya women wearing military uniforms instead of traditional dress and carting guns instead of babies. (Abdel-Moneim 1996)

Women are not just combatants within the EZLN, they also hold positions of political authority. One of the most recognized comandantes of the EZLN is Ramona, an indigenous woman who has often spoken on behalf of the Zapatistas. As one scholar notes, 'Ramona's presence in the media has helped focus the public's eye on women's issues in Mexico and abroad' (Goetze 1997a). But there are many other women involved in the EZLN.

For example, Subcomandante Marcos's *Our Word is Our Weapon* (2001b) begins with an essay entitled 'Twelve Women in the Twelfth Year: The Moment of War', which is an introduction to twelve women, some captains, some lieutenants, who led troops and fought for their lives on 1 January 1994.

Indigenous women have joined the armed struggle of the Zapatistas for a variety of reasons. On the one hand, many of the women have joined the army to escape the physical abuse and forced marriage suffered by women within the communities. One combatant, Isadora, admits that she had to join the army 'or else I'd die of the beatings from my uncle' (Goetze 1997b). On the other hand, women are drawn to the army because of the freedom and autonomy offered there. Women are not just given military training; they are also taught how to read and write in Spanish, and they learn the politics of the struggle and international laws (Stephen 2002: 182). Women also enjoy social rights in the army that they are not allowed in the communities. For example, female combatants have the right to choose their sexual partners and to access contraception, rights to which many civilian women in Chiapas have yet to achieve (Goetze 1997a). Of course, underneath these factors is the desire to join in the fight for liberation. As one combatant said, 'because we women are also oppressed ... we have organized ourselves together, men and women so that we can achieve what we want: peace, justice, dignity and the respect for the rights of men and women' (Stephen 2002: 186).

It is clear that many of the female combatants were drawn into the army not only to participate actively in the struggle, but also to gain autonomy and respect. The women often comment on the different opportunities available to them in the army. They are also pleased about the equal division of labour in the army, where the men are expected to do their share of cooking, cleaning, sewing; 'In the EZLN, everything is shared' (Perez and Castellanos 1994).

While much has been made about the visibility of women in the EZLN, feminists have questioned whether or not allowing women to join the army is consistent with trying to achieve real equality as any armed force tends to replicate the patriarchal modes of conflict resolution and power structures from which it comes (see Bedregal 1994; Abdel-Moneim 1996). Cynthia Enloe, a feminist scholar who works on issues of gender and the military, warns about the dangers of equating women's militarization with women's liberation. It is not unusual, she notes, for women to be welcomed into the military at a time of military need (1988: 99). The Zapatistas were, and are, in a position of need. Their numbers are quite limited, and without the women they would be even more limited. Enloe goes on to note that overcoming male resistance to women's inclusion in the military 'can persuade a progressive woman that she is taking a step towards liberation when she presses for inclusion in the military' (100).

However, whether the army is the perpetuation of patriarchal model or a new political possibility, indigenous women have used their position within the EZLN to fight for the rights of all women — 'They had used their empowerment from within the Army to form a new tool for creating equality between the genders in the communities' (Goetze 1997a). This new tool is the Women's Revolutionary Law, and the perspective on gender oppression that it represents has become a key feature of Zapatismo's rebel appeal as political philosophy and political practice.

The uprising began by the Zapatistas on 1 January 1994 was actually their second attempt at revolution. As Subcomandante Marcos would later relate, 'The first uprising of the EZLN was in March 1993 and it was led by the women Zapatistas. They suffered no losses and they won.' The women's 'challenge [to] the men of the EZLN with their own ideology of democracy, justice and liberty for all people' (Goetze 1997b) was not merely a challenge; it was, in the eyes of many, a revolution. This revolution began when the Zapatistas started to develop the laws of the revolution in preparation for their uprising. An insurgent named Major Susana was given the task of canvassing Zapatista women in the communities to see what kinds of laws they wanted to see implemented (Poniatowska 2002: 55). When Major Susana returned to report to the EZLN's revolutionary committee, she presented her findings to mixed reviews (55). The women applauded Susana, but the men 'simply looked at one another, nervous, distressed' (56). However, despite this initial hesitation, the proposals were unanimously passed and codified as the Women's Revolutionary Law, constituted as follows:

> In their just fight for the liberation of our people, the EZLN incorporates women into the revolutionary struggle regardless of their race, creed, color, or political affiliation, requiring only that they share the demands of the exploited people and that they commit to the laws and regulations of the revolution. In addition, taking into account the situation of the woman worker in Mexico, the revolution supports their just demands for equality and justice in the following Revolutionary Women's Law.
>
> First: Women, regardless of their race, creed, color, or political affiliation, have the right to participate in the revolutionary struggle in a way determined by their desire and ability.
>
> Second: Women have the right to work and receive a fair salary.
>
> Third: Women have the right to decide the number of children they will bear and care for.
>
> Fourth: Women have the right to participate in the affairs of the community and to hold positions of authority if they are freely and democratically elected.
>
> Fifth: Women and children have the right to primary attention in matters of health and nutrition.
>
> Sixth: Women have the right to education.

Seventh: Women have the right to choose their partner and are not to be forced into marriage.

Eighth: Women shall not be beaten or physically mistreated by their family members or by strangers. Rape and attempted rape will be severely punished.

Ninth: Women will be able to occupy positions of leadership in the organization and to hold military ranks in the revolutionary armed forces.

Tenth: Women will have all the rights and obligations elaborated in the revolutionary laws and regulations. (EZLN 1993)

But passing the laws is not the same thing as ensuring compliance with them. On the very day that the Revolutionary Women's Law was adopted, an indigenous man was heard saying:

'The good thing is that my wife doesn't understand Spanish, because if she did....' A female Tzotzil insurgent with the rank of major in the infantry started in at him: 'You're screwed, because we're going to translate it into all of our dialects.' The impertinent man could only lower his gaze. (Poniatowska 2002: 56)

Furthermore, these laws, which include women's right to work and to education, to choose who and when they marry and how many children they have, are not easily enforced in the communities. Despite the difficulties faced in actually implementing the Women's Revolutionary Law, the explicit awareness of gender oppression that it represents has been a foundational element of Zapatismo as political philosophy — if not always as practice — and a significant dimension of its rebel appeal, particularly transnationally.

If the indigenous of Chiapas occupy the most marginalized social rungs in Mexican society — living in extreme poverty, often without electricity and potable water, and dying far too often of curable disease — indigenous women bear the brunt of much of this suffering. Responsible for walking long distances to collect water and firewood, as well as for all the cooking, cleaning, washing and childcare, indigenous women work sixteen to eighteen hours a day, rising early to prepare food and turning in late after the embers have burned down, with no relief from the workload when sick or pregnant. In times of dire need women are expected to sacrifice their own resources to help their families. Indigenous women are considered the property of men; they suffer physical abuse from male relatives; girls are sold into marriage at a young age; and they have little, if any, education and are unlikely to speak Spanish. The leading cause of death among indigenous women is complications due to childbirth, and most women will have between seven and ten children (Goetze 1997a).

These conditions are further complicated by global relations. Research has shown that 'women and children have suffered disproportionately as a result of global economic restructuring' (Desai 2002: 32). This new global order is an inherently gendered one in which men are privileged 'in a variety of ways, such as unequal wages, unequal labour force participation, unequal structures of ownership and control of property, unequal control over one's body, as well as cultural and sexual privileges' (Kimmel 2003: 604). And some scholars have also argued that the introduction of capitalism into the indigenous communities has

> changed the pattern of gender relations. The complementary roles that characterize subsistence economies were displaced by more unequal relations. In this new economic context, indigenous women lost autonomy and began to depend on the salaries of their husbands or suffer a marginalized insertion into the capitalist market. (Hernández Castillo 1997: 104)

Pre-existing gender roles — which may have offered women more autonomy and equality, or at least more respect and better status — are challenged and complicated by a new capitalist economic system which prioritizes production and economic gains over sustainable, community-based living. However, there is considerable danger in romanticizing the dichotomy between the modern and the traditional. Indigenous traditions are not inherently equal, and the Zapatista women want to 'assert their rights to maintain cultural differences while, at the same time, demanding the right to change those traditions that oppress or exclude them' (Hernández Castillo 1997: 110). Indeed, as I have already sought to demonstrate in this chapter, the roots of Zapatismo lie in the critical, self-conscious and innovative approach to political process fashioned by migrant indigenous communities separated from their traditional contexts. In this same vein, Zapatista women want to address 'the indigenous essentialism that calls for an unquestioning defence of cultural traditions ... and reinvent [traditions] under new terms' (110).

Of course, it would be a critical error to imagine that the indigenous woman's life is filled with nothing but hardship. One journalist who spent several months living in a Zapatista community tells of how she came to understand that the indigenous women are also integral and respected members of their communities. Women are essential to the survival of the culture because they are the carriers of tradition. Women pass on the tradition to their daughters, who pass it to their daughters. The women are proud of their knowledge and skills and are 'dedicated to changing their own lives and those of their children for the better' (Clayton 1997). While this ideology allows women to be respected within a community, it also perpetuates the notion of 'women's work' and significantly limits the exercise of their individual autonomy. Women are respected as mothers, as caregivers, and as teachers; all activities that fall within the bounds of women's 'natural' attributes. This respect, although important, does not fundamentally challenge pre-existing gender roles.

The Women's Revolutionary Law, which demands the right to education, the right to choose a husband, and the right to be free from physical abuse, has occasionally been criticized by feminists because of its practical interests. Practical interests are 'usually a response to an immediate perceived need, and they do not generally entail a strategic goal such as women's emancipation or gender equality' (Goetze 1997a). However, this distinction between practical and strategic made by feminists can be seen as 'reflecting the ethnocentric views of feminists in North America and Europe' (Harvey 1998: 225), and other feminists have argued that strategic and practical goals are not exclusive, but work together to create real change. The challenge to practical, material problems in the communities is also a challenge to the 'gendered power relations that had traditionally subordinated women to men' (225).

Whether or not the Women's Revolutionary Law is feminist, or whether its goals are strategic or practical, it is a real challenge to dominant gender relations in many indigenous communities in Chiapas. In addition to this, these laws and the internal movement consultation they testify to, have served to advance Zapatismo as a rebel political philosophy and practice that is explicitly grappling with issues of gender oppression, something to which few movements transnationally can convincingly lay claim. The gender dynamics codified by the Zapatistas' Women's Revolutionary Law are far from perfect on the ground in Zapatista communities in Chiapas. Nevertheless, the existence of these laws and the spirit they speak to have added a compelling and vital gendered dynamic to the rebel appeal of the Zapatistas nationally and around the world.

To change the world without taking power

As a political philosophy and political practice Zapatismo emerges out of the lived reality within which it is situated. In this chapter, I have sought to trace the socio-historical roots of Zapatismo and to illuminate how its radical nature is truly only appreciable when situated in relation to the social, political and cultural context out of which it has been born. Within Mexico, the Zapatistas have been seen largely as rebels — with the legitimacy that implies — rather than as terrorists or criminals precisely because their struggle has been situated explicitly in relation to the lived realities that have constituted it. Transnationally, the Zapatista rebellion took on global significance because the Zapatistas identified globalized neoliberal capitalism as a force oppressing not only them but a multitude of others around the world as well. But beyond all of this, Zapatismo functions as rebel praxis because it embodies and seeks to provoke entirely new ways of thinking about and practising political possibility. In this regard, issues of power, democracy, autonomy and dignity are central to the Zapatista struggle and to Zapatismo as rebel philosophy and practice more broadly. As John Holloway, autonomist Marxist scholar and long-time Zapatista observer, asserts with respect to the challenge and promise of Zapatismo,

> What is at issue is not who exercises power, but how to create a world based on the mutual recognition of human dignity, on the formation of social relations which are not power relations ... This, then, is the revolutionary challenge at the beginning of the twenty-first century: to change the world without taking power. This is the challenge that has been formulated most clearly by the Zapatista uprising in the south-east of Mexico. (2002a: 17–20)

So does this mean that Zapatismo is a political theory or a particular type of social struggle complete with its own ideology? This question is best answered by examining some of the most essential dimensions of Zapatismo itself. In an interview in 2001, Subcomandante Marcos would reflect:

> our army is very different from others, because its proposal is to cease being an army. A soldier is an absurd person who has to resort

to arms in order to convince others, and in that sense the movement has no future if its future is military. If the EZLN perpetuates itself as an armed military structure, it is headed for failure. Failure as an alternative set of ideas, an alternative attitude to the world. … You cannot reconstruct the world or society, or rebuild national states now in ruins, on the basis of a quarrel over who will impose their hegemony on society. (García Márquez and Pombo 2004: 4–5)

Marcos elaborated on this point by noting that 'The EZLN has reached a point where it has been overtaken by Zapatismo', establishing the distance between Zapatismo and the EZLN (5). What does this mean? First, it means that Zapatismo is not identical with the EZLN. The EZLN is the Zapatista Army, which exists to defend the Zapatista communities in Chiapas, and is an army which is subordinated to the authority of the Zapatista communities themselves. This relationship is formally expressed through the Indigenous Revolutionary Clandestine Committee–General Command (CCRI–CG), which is composed of civilian Zapatista comandantes, who are in turn beholden to the authority of their respective community assemblies, a relationship that exemplifies the Zapatista slogan of 'to lead by obeying'.

A second dimension to the distinction Marcos identifies is that Zapatismo is not a coherent ideology; it is not a codified set of absolute rules, a platform, or a party line to which one can adhere. While I describe it as a 'political philosophy' here, it is also more than this. Marcos has called Zapatismo an 'intuition', a position elaborated upon by Manuel Callahan in the following way: 'Zapatismo is a political strategy, an ethos, a set of commitments claimed by those who claim a political identity' (2004b: 218–19). It is in this sense that Zapatismo can be said to embody an approach to politics based on the pursuit of 'democracy, liberty, and justice' — the banners of the Zapatista struggle from the moment of its public emergence — for all. What each of these terms means, of course, differs depending upon the space and place within which people find themselves, but in no case are they limited to liberal democratic understandings of them. While notions such as 'justice', 'democracy' and 'freedom' have been and continue to be used by a wide variety of political and economic power-holders, what distinguishes the discourse of Zapatismo from them is precisely its radical critique of power. Even within each specific context these meanings can never be fixed because such an assertion would be to claim a singular and transcendent truth, a notion which the Zapatistas reject. 'Walking questioning' is the Zapatista slogan which perhaps best embodies this commitment and expresses the belief that if one begins with answers and seeks to impose solutions, systems of power and domination are merely reproduced.

Within Zapatismo, the concepts of autonomy and interconnectedness are deeply intertwined. Autonomy — the capacity to govern oneself — is central because dignity is only possible when individuals and communities have both the freedom and the responsibility to govern themselves. Interconnectedness is the necessary complement to autonomy because a world that does not recognize existence as shared and interdependent is a world pitted against itself, a world doomed to replicate exclusion, division and violence. The challenge of creating a new world rooted in social relations that are not power relations and that emerge out of the mutual recognition of dignity is something the Zapatistas have undertaken most seriously. This refusal to claim a 'power over' and simultaneously the affirmation of a 'power to' create a world rooted in dignity, democracy, justice and liberty can thus be seen as embodying what Subcomandante Marcos means when he calls Zapatismo an 'intuition'.

The challenge of Zapatismo:
revolutionary action beyond insurgency

In the years since the EZLN rose up in arms, much has been made of the fact that this movement has not only managed to survive but has remained a significant force at the national and transnational levels. Clearly, this influence cannot be attributed to the military potential of the EZLN as their forces never truly posed a threat to the Mexican army. However, as I have sought to convey in this chapter, bullets have long since ceased to be the primary weapon of the Zapatistas. Instead, communicative action and the concrete building of alternatives have proven to be Zapatismo's most effective armaments. Unlike traditional guerrilla armies, which seek to achieve power by overthrowing the existing regime on the way to implementing a predefined socialist programme (see, for example, Guevara 1961), the Zapatistas' 'rebellion was … revelatory rather than programmatic' (Harvey 1998: 199). As Neil Harvey writes in his assessment of the Zapatista rebellion:

> Rather than emerging with a preconceived plan for revolutionary change, the Zapatistas represented the antithesis of such a vanguard. The cry of ¡Ya basta! was in fact a call for solidarity among all those Mexicans who had said 'enough is enough'. The precise nature of the demands could only result from a broader dialogue to which all those who recognized the need for change were invited … the EZLN also insisted on the centrality of democracy in articulating popular struggles against numerous forms of oppression. The EZLN looked beyond its own economic–corporate demands to the expansion of democratic political, social, and cultural practices in all spheres of Mexican life. Its strength therefore lay less with its own political and military resources and more in the changes that its presence effected in cultural understandings of democracy and citizenship (199).

The Zapatistas have not survived either physically or politically through society's altruistic interest in them; instead, they have survived due to their engagement of the people of Mexico and, often, the world in an imaginative project not only of social reconstruction but of ideological and conceptual rebirth as well. The Zapatista struggle has thus not been for 'authentic' democracy, justice and liberty, but for a fundamental reconsideration of what those very terms mean, something that ultimately can only occur within an open and unfolding process of dialogue and engagement.

The Zapatistas are significant in relation to the history of guerrilla movements because since the early days of 1994 their revolutionary struggle has been waged both through the concrete building of autonomy in the Mexican south-east and in the minds of people — in Mexico and around the world. At the national level, the Zapatista movement has subverted the very assumptions upon which the ruling elite in Mexico had founded their power and authority. Transnationally, the Zapatistas put the radical possibility of social, economic and political alternatives to the status quo back on the table after neoliberal ideologues had attempted to foreclose upon them. The rebel challenges Zapatismo has made to the ideological supports for dominant social, political and economic systems are central to the lived struggle the Zapatistas have waged in an attempt to provide the possibility of articulating and crystallizing new social and political spaces.

An important dimension to this struggle against dominant ideologies is the conception of 'the nation' within Zapatismo. Throughout their struggle, the Zapatistas have continually asserted not only the indigenous nature of their movement, but its Mexicanness as well. The Zapatistas as a guerrilla army are one of *national liberation*. Thus their agenda and their demands are not limited to the indigenous communities of Chiapas or even to the state itself; rather, they are national in nature. Indeed, this national emphasis in Zapatista discourse has often been viewed problematically — or ignored entirely — by radicals and other observers from outside of Mexico, and particularly those from the global north. Conflated either with a petty nationalist chauvinism or an empty social-democratic rhetoric, Carolina Ballesteros Corona and Patrick Cuninghame have argued that these criticisms fail

> to understand the EZLN's concept of nationhood based on a network of autonomous communities rather than the historically centralised, hierarchical nation-state. Nor do they appreciate the originality of its strategy for revolutionary transformation to a post-capitalist society which is based not on a vanguardist seizure of the state and the commanding heights of the economy, let alone parliamentary reformism, but on an alliance with other grassroots social movements. (1998: 16)

The Zapatista struggle is indeed a national one, but not in terms of an affirmation of the singular, elite-driven project of the 'nation-state'. Notions of autonomy, direct and voluntary participation, and dialogue are quite clearly evident here and it is upon this foundation that Zapatismo as rebel political philosophy and practice is constructed.

From the moment the rebellion began, Zapatista discourse has been deeply marked by three primary concepts: democracy, liberty and justice. Among the central demands of the EZLN in justifying their rebellion to the Mexican people in the 'First Declaration of the Lacandón Jungle', their declaration of war, these words would also always accompany the closure and official signature on Zapatista communiqués. In constantly invoking them, the Zapatistas not only fought under their banner; they also fought *for* these concepts and, often, for their radicalization beyond liberal notions of individual rights. While the call for 'democracy' clearly resonated with Mexicans, who had been subject to single-party rule for the past seven decades, the Zapatista notion of 'democracy' goes far beyond electoral politics and effective suffrage.

Following the victory of Vicente Fox of the National Action Party in the presidential elections of July 2000, it was widely declared that the Zapatistas must have achieved what they wanted: the defeat of the PRI and the democratization of the political system. This severely limited conception of democracy — the ritualized transfer of power among a very small group of elites — stands in stark contrast to the direct democracy of the Zapatistas. The Zapatista conceptualization of democracy is rooted in the capacity of individuals not only to participate in a political system, but to determine the very nature of it. While an end to fraudulent electoral practices is certainly a useful first step, the Zapatista conceptualization of 'democracy' rests upon 'the application at all levels of society of the direct participatory democracy of the local assembly, involving collective and inclusive decision-making based on consensus rather than voting' (Ballesteros Corona and Cuninghame 1998: 17). Fundamentally, democracy for the Zapatistas is 'people's power', a phrase which conveys the essential notion that people themselves have the ultimate authority over the manner in which their lives should be lived. Gustavo Esteva reflects on this construction of 'democracy' within Zapatista discourse in the following manner:

> people's power is but the translation of the Greek word for democracy, from *demos* — the people, the commons, and *kratos* — force, power, rule. For those who constitute 'the people', democracy is a matter of common sense: that ordinary people govern their own lives. It does not allude to a kind of government, but to a government end. It is not a collection of institutions, but an historical project. With the word of democracy, people are not alluding to present democracies, already existing or being established, but to the thing itself, to people's power. (1999: 154)

From this perspective democracy is not about institutions; it is about a collective, relational practice. The concept of the collective is central in relation to the Zapatista rebel subject. Rather than seeing the individual as the primary locus of radical social, political and economic change, in Zapatismo it is the community. But instead of subsuming or erasing individual difference within the collective, Zapatismo celebrates individual autonomy within the web of interdependencies that is human existence — a state of being embodied by the democratic community. In this context, democracy is a certain type of relation between people and the capacity to determine the course and nature of their lives. As rebels on a national and transnational stage, the Zapatistas have contributed greatly to a renewed discussion of a direct and deepened democracy and what it might mean to be an active subject engaged in such a collective practice.

The second concept appearing alongside the Zapatista call for 'democracy' is 'liberty'. While it may appear that 'liberty' is a fairly self-evident concept, much like 'democracy', it should not be assumed that it is as simple a notion as one might suppose. As Ballesteros Corona and Cuninghame remark in their analysis of this concept:

> For the Zapatistas, freedom means autonomy and self-determination and in the context of Chiapas, indigenous autonomy and self-determination within the confines of the Mexican national territory. This desire and need for autonomy implies the right to self-organise society according to the needs, customs and practices of the immediate local community, rather than submit to a form of government formerly imposed by the centralised nation-state and now by the global interests of neoliberal capital. (1998: 17)

'Liberty' or 'freedom' does not simply imply the absence of limits, but rather the capacity to act according to one's own needs within a space that is necessarily shared with others. Similar to the

conception of 'democracy', the Zapatista notion of 'liberty' conveys
a very autonomous but interconnected sense of decision-making.
Rather than a freedom from something, this concept expresses
the freedom to engage in action based on self-determination and
democratic decision-making processes. This notion is clearly
reflected in the Zapatista emphasis on democratic dialogue and
engagement, as these formations and interactions are only possible
if people possess the freedom to engage in such associations.
Furthermore, the concept of 'liberty' here not only refers to
the ability to engage in diverse social action and relationships,
but to have the freedom to determine what form these acts and
relationships should take and what ends they should be directed
towards. This point is exemplified by a comment made by Subcomandante Marcos during an interview with Medea Benjamin.
In response to a question regarding whether the sacrifices made
by the Zapatistas would be in vain if a right-wing political party
were to come to power, Marcos replied: 'We want to create the
political space, and we want the people to have the education
and the political maturity to make good choices' (Benjamin 1995:
61). Thus, conceptions of democracy, liberty and political space
are all fundamentally interconnected for the Zapatistas. Liberty
is therefore characterized as the essential capacity for people to
be able to choose freely for themselves what kind of life they
want to live and the manner in which they wish to live it. This
choice, however, is never a purely selfish one; it is also one that
is clearly situated in relation to those with whom we share the
world. While autonomy cannot be abridged, it necessarily exists in
a state of tension and interdependence with respect to the mutual
obligations and responsibilities that constitute lived existence.

The third 'cornerstone' concept of Zapatismo is that of 'justice'.
Once more, this concept is at once profoundly ambiguous in
its broadness and deceiving in its apparent simplicity. Much

like 'democracy' and 'liberty' this word conveys a very specific conception of what 'justice' means for the Zapatista movement. Within the Zapatista movement, 'justice' is

> synonymous with dignity and respect for indigenous cultures and ways of life, indeed for all 'differences' within Mexico, linking up with the demands of the women's and gay movements. It also means an end to the impunity of the PRI regime, the punishment of its appalling human rights abuses and the endemic corruption of its 'narco-political' alliance with business, military and organized crime elites. Ultimately, justice for the EZLN means social and economic justice in a post-capitalist society. (Ballesteros Corona and Cuninghame 1998: 17–18)

The Zapatistas' notion of 'justice' is not simply a demand for the just application of the law or even the reformation of the legal system but rather for a society within which dignity and respect are the primary standards according to which people are treated. The Zapatista conceptions of democracy, liberty and justice rest upon a perspective which views the world as a place characterized by multiplicity and diversity, a perspective which in fact is brilliantly articulated by the Zapatista slogan 'queremos un mundo donde quepan muchos mundos' — 'we want a world which holds many worlds' (Navarro 1998: 162). For a society to be 'just', it must not only view difference as legitimate, but acknowledge that difference and radical multiplicity are essential characteristics of existence rather than notions to be merely tolerated.

In fact, the Zapatista emphasis on 'equality' is another concept closely aligned with 'justice' in that it is an explicit denial of any attempts to standardize or homogenize people. Rather than implying standardization, equality is instead the appreciation and respect for difference, the appreciation and respect for autonomy. Justice, as with equality, is a concept which resides not in the identification of people with a single notion of the 'individual'

or the 'citizen' but in the recognition of the profound differences which exist among, between and within people. In his
examination of the Zapatista conception of equality, Gustavo
Esteva articulates a number of points which apply equally to the
Zapatista notion of justice:

> People are not homogeneous and even less equals. They are hetero-
> geneous and different. The illusion of equality, which now operates
> as a popular prejudice, became an ideal under specific historical
> circumstances, to struggle against power abuses and people's desti-
> tution. It now operates as a continual source of illegitimate privileges
> and inequality. The Zapatistas denounce the illusory character of
> this ideal, recognize personal and collective differences and claim
> people's power, for the end of privilege and license. They also affirm
> the assumption of the diversity of all peoples and cultures, whose
> interaction should occur on equal footing, that is, with no implicit or
> explicit assumption of the superiority of any culture over the others,
> in order to establish the harmonious coexistence of the 'different'.
> (1999: 157)

A just society does not seek to erase differences or create an
environment of equality through structural or legalistic imposi-
tions. Instead, a society is just when it explicitly recognizes the
differences inherent in people and yet disavows any hierarchy
of difference. For all of these notions, respect for autonomy and
difference remains the central concept. For the Zapatistas, a new
society is only possible through the engagement of multiple and
diverse members of that society with each other. Difference is not
only acknowledged but in fact a necessary and integral component
for the visualization and articulation of a new world.

The politics of 'no'

What some have called the 'politics of no' are of central importance to both the Zapatista rebellion and the movement which

grew out of it. At its core, the 'politics of no' emerges from the fact that the Zapatistas have continually asserted their disavowal of any aspirations to seize power and impose a unitary vision of revolutionary change on everyone else. Fernanda Navarro remarks on this unique perspective on power in the Zapatista struggle in the following manner:

> Marcos has said that 'the only virtue of Power is that, in the end, it inevitably produces a revolution against itself'. History has taught us that even in outstanding cases when tyranny or dictatorships were overthrown by revolutionary liberating forces, disillusionment sooner or later follows when we witness that the basic principles of justice and freedom, which led the struggle, begin to decay. It is as if there were some dominating traits inherent to power itself which gradually end up in a repetition, resemblance, or reproduction of — not an alternative to — the rigid, arbitrary governments which were overthrown. (1998: 161)

When the Zapatistas say 'no' to the seizure of power, what they are simultaneously affirming is the necessity of the creation of a new kind of political space not limited to conventional notions of revolution. In the words of John Holloway, 'The revolutions of the twentieth century failed because they aimed too low, not because they aimed too high' (2002b: 158). The state is simply not enough because relations of domination, control and exploitation are not limited to it. As Holloway asserts, we need a new conception of revolution and a new kind of radical politics, one in which dignity operates as a central concept. 'If dignity is taken as a central principle, then people cannot be treated as means: the creation of a society based on dignity can only take place through the development of social practices based on the mutual recognition of that dignity' (159). Dialogue and engagement are only possible among members of a society who do not wish to dominate or rule over one another, so Zapatismo fundamentally rejects the notion of the seizure of power.

In declaring ';Ya basta!' — 'enough!' — and in declaring 'no' to
the seizure of power, what the Zapatistas have done is to set the
stage for the involvement of multiple groups and individuals to
participate in their own ways and according to their own terms in
a collective articulation of discontent. As opposed to attempting to
subsume difference and multiplicity beneath an all-encompassing
ideology, the Zapatistas have instead asserted their own struggle
in all of its historical, geographical and socio-political specificity.
This is why each communiqué and declaration is signed 'from the
mountains of the Mexican south-east' — it is an assertion of locality and particularity, of difference and heterogeneity. Similarly,
the Zapatistas have encouraged others to articulate their own
struggles in their own terms and according to their own histories.
Rather than articulating a single position or attempting to unite
people beneath a single monolithic, hegemonic structure, the
Zapatistas have instead sought to create space for the articulation
of multiple visions and discourses.

Gustavo Esteva notes with regard to the politics of 'no' that this
approach distinguishes itself by allowing 'the new coalitions of
discontents to affirm themselves in their own local spaces, while
widening their social and political force to promote their localized
views and interests' (1999: 161). The concept of autonomy is
central to this political stance as groups and individuals are not
only allowed but encouraged to express their particular agendas
and interests. Rather than the standardization and homogeniza-
tion that representative democratic governments espouse and
exemplify, the politics of 'no' expresses multiplicity, dynamism
and difference. In the words of Gustavo Esteva:

> To say 'no' may be the most complete and vigorous way of affirma-
> tion. The unifying 'no', expressing a shared opposition, usually
> conveys multiple 'yes'es: the affirmations of what all those sharing
> a rejection want. The organization around what people don't want,

avoiding the condensation of their diverse affirmations, recognizes such plurality ... Politicians and parties, in contrast, always in need of followers, find it impossible or ineffective to focus themselves on the 'no'. They continually look for affirmative proposals, defining homogenous and abstract ideals or wants. (161)

The Zapatistas have been criticized by some for not possessing or expressing a concrete agenda or plan for the future of the Mexican nation. What those who make such criticisms fail to understand is that the Zapatistas do not espouse such a vision because such a project needs to be the product of dialogue and engagement among all members of society. To do otherwise would be to betray the essence of the Zapatista struggle for political space, for 'an antechamber looking onto a new world'. In this sense, by declaring 'no', the Zapatistas actually affirm a space and a relationship of fundamental inclusiveness, a space which is rebellious, radically democratic, engaged, multiple, heterogeneous and even antagonistic.

3

'Never again a Mexico without us'

THE NATIONAL IMPACT
OF ZAPATISMO

On 1 JANUARY 1994, the EZLN fundamentally altered the political landscape in Mexico by rising up in arms and declaring war on the Mexican army and the federal executive. However, in the days, weeks, months and years that would follow in the Zapatistas' war against oblivion, an unexpected yet equally important force would enter into the struggle declared by the Zapatistas — Mexican civil society. With no pre-existing connections to the EZLN, in the days following the uprising people from across Mexico would mobilize to support the Zapatista demands, bring a halt to the government counteroffensive, and call for a path to social change other than that of armed revolution. As Zapatista leaders would later recount, having spent a decade preparing themselves for war, the insurgents and base communities of the EZLN now had to learn how to engage an entirely different scenario. The encounter between the Zapatistas and diverse members of Mexican civil society would not only reshape the nature of the EZLN's insurgency; it would also reshape the political landscape in Mexico itself.

While observers outside of Mexico have often made much of the Zapatistas' influence upon the transnational fabric of political action — particularly in relation to its influence upon the alter-globalization 'movement of movements' — the most tangible and enduring effects of Zapatismo have been felt in the local, regional and national contexts the movement occupies. The number of actions undertaken by the Zapatistas to engage Mexican civil society since 1994 is extensive and it is not the intention of this book to provide an exhaustive list of these initiatives. Instead, what I aim to provide in this chapter is an overview of Zapatismo's impact within Mexico since the beginning of the rebellion.

Zapatismo and rebel Mexico

In 'A Storm and a Prophecy — Chiapas: The Southeast in Two Winds', a communiqué written to the Mexican people two years before the uprising but not issued publicly until 27 January 1994, Zapatista spokesperson Subcomandante Insurgente Marcos takes the reader on a trip through Chiapas, Mexico. Written in the form of a morbid travel guide, Marcos outlines the case for rebellion as he illuminates the realities of life in one of the poorest states in Mexico:

Chiapas loses blood through many veins: through oil and gas ducts, electric lines, railways; through bank accounts, trucks, vans, boats and planes; through clandestine paths, gaps, and forest trails. This land continues to pay tribute to the imperialists: petroleum, electricity, cattle, money, coffee, banana, honey, corn, cacao, tobacco, sugar, soy, melon, sorghum, mamey, mango, tamarind, avocado, and Chiapaneco blood all flow as a result of the thousand teeth sunk into the throat of the Mexican Southeast. These raw materials, thousands of millions of tons of them, flow to Mexican ports and railroads, air and truck transportation centers. From there they are sent to different parts of the world — the United States, Canada, Holland,

Germany, Italy, Japan — but all to fulfill one same destiny: to feed imperialism. Since the beginning, the fee that capitalism imposes on the southeastern part of this country oozes blood and mud. (2001a: 22–3)

The reality of life in Chiapas is that it produces a great deal, both for Mexico and for trading partners around the world, but the lives of its inhabitants — particularly its indigenous inhabitants — are not advantaged by this exchange. In fact, the more lucrative these resources become within a globalized market, the more marginalized the indigenous inhabitants of this state have become. Marcos continues his narrative by asking, 'What does the beast leave behind in exchange for all it takes away?', and he responds:

Half of [the rural inhabitants of Chiapas] don't have potable water, and two-thirds have no sew[er]age service. Ninety per cent of the rural population pays little or no taxes.

Communication in Chiapas is a grotesque joke for a state that produces petroleum, electricity, coffee, wood, and cattle for the hungry beast. Only two-thirds of the municipal seats have paved-road access. Twelve thousand communities have no other means of transport and communication than mountain trails. ...

And education? It is the worst in the country. At the elementary school level, 72 out of every 100 children don't finish the first grade. More than half of the schools only offer up to a third-grade education, and half of the schools only have one teacher for all the courses offered. There are statistics, although they are kept secret of course, that show that many indigenous children are forced to drop out of school due to their families' need to incorporate them into the system of exploitation. In any indigenous community it is common to see children carrying corn and wood, cooking, or washing clothes during school hours....

The health conditions of the people of Chiapas are a clear example of the capitalist imprint: 1.5 million people have no medical services at their disposal. There are 0.2 clinics for every 1,000 inhabitants, one-fifth the national average. There are 0.3 hospital beds for every 1,000 Chiapanecos, one-third the amount in the rest of Mexico. There is one operating room per 100,000 inhabitants, one-half of the amount in the rest of Mexico. There are 0.5 doctors and 0.4 nurses per 1,000 people, one-half of the national average.

... the Southeast continues to export raw materials, just as it did 500 years ago. It continues to import capitalism's principal product: death and misery. (2001a: 24–5)

Marcos's morbid travelogue paints a grim picture of exploitation, neglect and systemic violence in Chiapas. The extremity and legitimacy of the grievances articulated in these passages deeply informed the way the Zapatistas' rebellion was perceived by others. Rather than bursting onto the national and international scene as the 'professionals of violence' they were initially accused of being by Mexican political elites, the Zapatista rebellion represented in the eyes of many an authentic uprising of the dispossessed. The legitimacy of the grievances underlying the rebellion and the way in which the rebellion itself was carried out were among the most important factors animating the response of Mexican civil society to the Zapatistas.

Looking back at the Zapatista uprising, Mexican scholar Gustavo Esteva speaks to the radical content it expressed, arguing that

The [Zapatista] uprising quickly offered an alternative to the national political agenda, once more bringing popular tradition and the customs of the elite into a confrontation to define the political future. Far from proposing a return to the regime inherited from the revolution, the impetus that the EZLN unleashed was oriented toward obtaining what that regime and all the previous ones had proved incapable of achieving: a social pact with effective participation by everyone, a social project based on the plurality of the peoples and cultures that make up Mexico and the diversity of their ideals. (2003: 247–8)

Expanding upon the political opening offered by the Zapatista rebellion and the radically inclusive nature of their struggle, anthropologist Xóchitl Leyva Solano explains how the Zapatistas have been able to create ties with what she refers to as 'Rebel Mexico'. 'Rebel Mexico', according to Leyva Solano, includes 'traditional parties of the left and centre-left, cells of clandestine political organisations and "legal" peasant, indigenous and sector organisations together with non-governmental organisations and civil associations' (1998: 38). The bases for identification between Zapatismo and Rebel Mexico include: worsening living conditions for people throughout Mexico; the entrenchment of ruling party power and privilege; the fragmentation of the organized left and its electoral defeat through massive fraud in 1988; and, finally, the widespread rejection of armed insurgency as a path to meaningful and lasting social change. Leyva Solano argues that the Zapatista rebellion had such significance within Mexico because it came at a particularly delicate time — just as the country was preparing to enter into the North American Free Trade Agreement with the US and Canada and to engage in yet another ritual of PRI presidential succession masquerading as an election (38). She also asserts that the 'convergence of different political actors' which came out of the Zapatista uprising was not an accidental or peripheral outcome 'since the EZLN discourse had always emphasised the necessity of fomenting ties between the various popular struggles that had taken place in Mexico, in "isolated nuclei", over the past five decades' (48).

The making of connections and the struggle over the meaning of social life are central aspects to appreciating the influence of Zapatismo within Mexico. While the original goal of the EZLN was to topple the Salinas government, defeat the Mexican military and establish the space necessary for people to restore democracy, liberty and justice to their own lives, the seizure of state power or the imposition of a unitary revolutionary programme were never part of the EZLN's aspirations. In participating in opening up democratic spaces where others could also engage in the pursuit of democracy and social justice in Mexico, the Zapatistas 'established a cultural strategy that called into question the PRI's hegemony by reinterpreting national symbols and discourses in favor of an alternative transformative project' (Gilbreth and Otero 2001: 9). Since the first days of the rebellion, the Zapatistas have striven to communicate the possibility that things could be radically different if people work to make them so, not in order to simply recapture a stolen revolutionary tradition but to make room for a future that has not been foreclosed upon.

But why did Zapatismo have such significance for diverse sectors of Mexican society? Why, instead of provoking panic and calls for a militarily imposed 'order', did Mexicans reach out to embrace it? Adolfo Gilly provides critical illumination as to why this unexpected encounter between an armed insurgency and a broad and amorphous civil society occurred. Gilly considers what he calls the 'adoption and protection' of the Zapatistas by Mexican civil society to be based upon seven central points. The first element that drew Mexican civil society to the Zapatistas was the nationally transmitted image of columns of armed and masked indigenous men and women taking control of the old colonial capital of San Cristóbal de las Casas. According to Gilly, this evoked 'the historical memory of the country, the memory transmitted in families or studied in school. Indians, those about whom the urban society bore an ancient and unconfessed guilt, had organized themselves and risen up with weapons in their hands' (1998: 309). Through these images and their transmission, 'In a single blow the rebellion had legitimated itself before Mexicans' (309). The second element, related to the first, is that the word 'Zapatismo' instantly explained the nature of the rebellion to the nation in 'terms accessible to all' (309). In a nation awash in revolutionary symbolism and history, the reclaimed legacy of Emiliano Zapata requires no explanation. Furthermore, the movement's right to claim this name and its history — one so often co-opted by ruling elites — was testified to by the fact that 'entire Indian communities had organized an army', embodying both the grassroots and autonomous legacy of the original Zapatista struggle (309). With the legitimacy of the rebellion established, Gilly argues the third element facilitating this unanticipated encounter came out of the Mexican government's negotiation with the Zapatistas. As he explains, 'One doesn't negotiate because one has the right to, but because one has the force to make that right recognized', a principle 'rooted in the common culture within which the Mexican state community has sustained itself, above all since the revolution of 1910' (309–10). By rising up in rebellion against the corrupt elements of the Mexican state, the Zapatistas did not approach the dominant power structure as clients asking for reforms; they approached it antagonistically, demanding it address the grievances levelled against it or fall completely in the face of this challenge. For Mexicans who had grown cynical about the ritual of official politics and the inability — or lack of interest — of governing elites to address their daily struggles, the Zapatista rebellion embodied a collective desire for radical change made by the people themselves.

The fourth basis explaining the attraction of the Zapatista rebellion for Mexican civil society is linked to the Zapatistas' core demands disseminated to Mexicans in the 'First Declaration of the Lacandón Jungle', the Zapatista declaration of war. The basic justness of these demands — work, land, housing, food, health care, education, independence, freedom, democracy, justice and peace — spoke not to a movement aiming to impose a revolution upon the rest of society but to one committed to participating in the creation of a social order based on principles of social justice for all. Further to this, the Zapatistas' invocation of Article 39 of the Mexican Constitution — stating that it is the inalienable right of Mexicans to change their government at any time — as the legal basis for their rebellion, and their call for the removal of the government of Carlos Salinas to allow for free and democratic elections to occur demonstrated to society at large that the Zapatistas did not want to destroy the Mexican state but sought 'rather to replace the existing political regime and its economic policy with another' (310). From the outset of the rebellion, it was clear that the Zapatistas did not want to subvert the Mexican state, instead, they wanted to reinvigorate it with a spirit of deep inclusivity and radical democracy while participating in reclaiming it from elite interests and giving it back to the Mexican people themselves.

The fifth basis explaining the importance of Zapatismo to Mexican civil society is linked to the Zapatistas' role in galvanizing a renewed and independent indigenous movement in Mexico, materialized in the form of the National Indigenous Congress (Gilly 1998: 310). Indeed, the Zapatista movement has brought unprecedented national attention to what many observers have called the 'Indian Question' in Mexico, generating debate about the conditions of life and the possibilities for indigenous peoples living within the Mexican state (Aridjis 2002; Gilly 1998; Mattiace 1997; Monsiváis 2002). By raising the 'Indian Question', the Zapatistas and the independent indigenous movement have stimulated a national debate concerning issues of autonomy, culture, and the historical and ongoing debt owed by colonial states to indigenous peoples. Gilly considers this moment to be marked by a 'diversification and democratization of Mexican political culture' that is entirely new and to which other broad sectors of Mexican society could relate (1998: 310–11).

If this was all the Zapatistas accomplished it would be a significant outcome in and of itself; however, in addition the Zapatistas
have also succeeded in galvanizing a broad range of democratic
movements in Mexico through innovative political projects and
encounters. In the words of Luis Hernández Navarro, 'among
the most important consequences of the Zapatista movement in
our times is that it has stimulated dreams of social change, and
resisted the idea that all emancipatory projects must be sacrificed
to global integration', and it did so through 'the symbolic force of
the image of armed revolution that still holds sway for many parts
of the population' and 'the moral force that indigenous struggles have acquired' (2002: 64–5). Furthermore, once 'the cult of
the rifles' had worn off what remained so appealing about the
Zapatistas was the very fact that they continued to articulate and
build a new political project. This clearly links to what Adolfo
Gilly identifies as the sixth basis explaining the significance of
the Zapatistas in the national context: namely, that they put the
issue of national identity and self-determination back on the
public agenda 'during a period when that notion was (once again)
the subject of debate', particularly in light of NAFTA and other
globalizing forces (1998: 311). The Zapatistas were not calling for
the abandonment of the Mexican nation; instead they called for
a rigorous re-examination of this national identity, specifically
who it excluded and who it privileged.

The final point identified by Gilly explaining the 'adoption
and protection' of the Zapatistas by Mexican civil society is the
dynamic communicative ability of the Zapatistas, their manage-
ment of modern media, and their profoundly original discourse.
The Zapatistas' way of communicating, Gilly contends, is so
powerful because it is articulated in a language 'of modern images
and ancient symbols, [which] does not propose a return to a past
either distant or near', instead suggesting 'the possibility of a

nonexcluding modernity, one that does not destroy history and those who carry it with them but, rather, integrates them into a reality where none are excluded' (1998: 312). The Zapatistas' strategy of engaging in a protracted dialogue with other rebels both near and far is predicated on the understanding that there is no one path to social justice. They do not romanticize some imagined past utopia; nor do they suggest that a future utopia is attainable. The Zapatistas have not asserted that doing away with all the trappings of the modern world is necessary to return to a socially just way of living. Instead, they have continually insisted that a world capable of holding many worlds — a world that is just, free, democratic and inclusive, as well as diverse and heterogeneous — can be built through committed collective action grounded in an awareness of the fact that there are a multitude of specific and different struggles against injustice and oppression. The Zapatistas have repeatedly affirmed that they do not have *the answer* to social change and that their struggle is not the leading edge of the movement for it. Their way of communicating both with the wider world and within Mexico has reaffirmed and embodied all these principles, and has operated as a central point upon which the appeal of Zapatismo has been based.

Ultimately, the significance of Zapatismo and the Zapatista rebellion rests upon the central pillar of the Zapatista movement itself — 'the material, human, and historical substance of this rebellion: the indigenous communities and the Indian leadership of the movement, without which the combination [of factors] would be impossible' (Gilly 1998: 312). Why have the Zapatistas been received as rebels fighting for just causes rather than as terrorists or other 'professionals of violence'? Quite simply because the movement is undeniably an organic expression of the most marginalized, oppressed and exploited peoples in Mexico. The fact that they have taken ownership of a struggle that directly and unapologetically confronts the elements of a political, economic and militarized system that seeks to deny them their very existence, while at the same time diligently and humbly working to forge connections with other Mexicans facing their own struggles, is the root of why the Zapatistas have been widely valorized as rebels.

As for Subcomandante Marcos's role in all of this, Gilly summarizes it well, stating that Marcos 'knew enough, first, to comprehend and assimilate that substance [of the indigenous communities] and, then, how to be the mediator or the guide through which its image is transmitted to urban society' (Gilly 1998: 312; also see Higgins 2000). Through a complex interplay of cultural, historical and political points of reference, a deep grounding in the indigenous communities from which it emerged, a communicative approach both profoundly shaped by the Mayan lifeworlds of southern Mexico and yet capable of speaking compellingly to diverse audiences, and a political project which challenges relations of power and domination while enriching democracy and reinvigorating the Mexican nation, the Zapatistas have galvanized 'Rebel Mexico' in a collective struggle not to conquer the world but to remake it.

Of course, none of this should be taken as suggesting that the Zapatista struggle has resulted in unqualified democratic gains. In fact, as several scholars have pointed out, the Zapatista movement has had a range of less than ideal effects, including exacerbating tensions in and between indigenous communities in Chiapas, and actually inhibiting significant pre-existing systems of community and municipal autonomy (Cal y Mayor 2003; Eber 2003; Gilbreth and Otero 2001; Leyva Solano 2003; Mattiace 2003). Nevertheless, the Zapatista rebellion was seen by many as 'a bold statement by an oppressed minority against an encroaching global capitalism that threatened the small Mayan farmer and, by extension, any subordinate group unable to shoulder the weight of global competition' (Gilbreth and Otero 2001: 18). Furthermore, in the face of this 'encroaching global system', the Zapatistas have not proposed an isolationist retreat from the world, a return to old social pacts, or a simple change of current power-holders for new ones. Instead, they have sought to realize 'a social project based on the plurality of the peoples and cultures that make up Mexico and the diversity of their ideals' (Esteva 2003: 248). By challenging ruling elites and the dominant political and economic power structure through concrete acts of creation and resistance, as well as through communicative acts aimed at subverting and demystifying the socio-cultural and historical mythology of power, the Zapatistas have prised open new spaces of political struggle and revitalized the desire to create truly democratic and inclusive alternatives. They have sought to engage, in their own words, in a project of building 'a world capable of holding many worlds'.

'From the mountains of the Mexican southeast': Zapatismo's politics of the word and the deed

Up to this point, I have sought to uncover the bases of Zapatismo's rebel appeal and significance within Mexico. Here, I turn to some of the concrete political effects generated by the Zapatistas in Mexico since 1994. My intention is not to be exhaustive. Instead, I seek to illuminate the significance of the Zapatista struggle in a national context by attending to some of the movement's key moments. While Zapatismo may be more 'intuition' than ideology, as a rebel political philosophy and practice there are nevertheless developments and points of reference that serve to provide a rough guide to it. While the Zapatistas, and particularly their spokesperson Subcomandante Marcos, have been nothing less

than prolific in their production of communiqués, denunciations and declarations since their New Year's Day uprising, none
are more significant than the six 'Declarations of the Lacandón
Jungle' in terms of outlining the evolving contours of Zapatismo
and the Zapatista struggle.

Using the declarations as a way to trace the development of
Zapatismo, it is important to realize that the core dynamic behind
the Zapatista struggle following the ceasefire declared by the
Mexican government on 12 January 1994 has been dialogue. While
this statement may seem strange given the fact that the EZLN
remains an armed insurgent force, the Zapatista movement has
moved beyond these beginnings to become something much
larger, much more diverse and, ultimately, much more powerful.
Through their emphasis upon dialogue and political space, the
Zapatistas have rooted their struggle in the concept of engagement with other actors involved in challenging an oppressive
and exploitive system. The basis for this engagement is, quite
simply, the word. It is through the words of their spokesperson,
Subcomandante Marcos, that the Zapatistas have been able to
reach beyond the borders of their geographic locality to engage
people around the world. It is through the careful deliberations
of their community assemblies that the Zapatistas have guided
their struggle and remained true to the radically democratic
nature of their alternative to the status quo. It is through their
emphasis upon communication and respectful dialogue that the
Zapatistas have managed to articulate the possibility of a common
struggle among so many diverse social actors. As Subcomandante
Marcos explains in the Zapatista communiqué 'The Word and
the Silence':

> What matters is our eldest elders who received the word and the
> silence as a gift in order to know themselves and to touch the heart
> of the other. Speaking and listening is how true men and women

learn to walk. It is the word that gives form to that walk that goes on inside of us. It is the word that is the bridge to cross to the other side. Silence is what Power offers our pain in order to make us small. When we are silenced, we remain very much alone. Speaking, we heal the pain. Speaking, we accompany one another. Power uses the word to impose his empire of silence. We use the word to renew ourselves. Power uses silence to hide his crimes. We use silence to listen to one another, to touch one another, to know one another.

This is the weapon, brothers and sisters. We say, the word remains. We speak the word. We shout the word. We raise the word and with it break the silence of our people. We kill the silence, by living the word. Let us leave Power alone in what the lie speaks and hushes. Let us join together in the word and the silence which liberate. (2001d: 84)

'The word', in this sense, conveys the radically emancipatory possibilities embodied in the act of speaking and listening to one another; it also conveys the fundamental and profoundly subversive power which resides in the capacity and willingness to communicate. Since the first days of 1994, the Zapatistas have maintained an uneasy ceasefire with the Mexican military while engaging in some profoundly innovative and creative actions in order to realize their own demands, as well as to galvanize actors nationally and transnationally in an attempt to create a broad front of resistance 'for humanity and against neoliberalism'. In so doing, they have articulated a vision of political possibility as unique as their struggle has been.

'Today we say enough is enough!' The Zapatistas declare war

The 'First Declaration of the Lacandón Jungle' was one of the first Zapatista documents released to the Mexican people following the uprising on the first day of January in 1994. It is, in its

most essential form, a declaration of war and a call to others to
join the Zapatista Army of National Liberation in this struggle.
The declaration begins with a historical contextualization of the
uprising and an assertion of the legitimacy of the action:

> To the people of Mexico
>
> Mexican brothers and sisters:
>
> We are a product of five hundred years of struggle: first, led by
> insurgents against slavery during the War of Independence with
> Spain; then to avoid being absorbed by North American imperial-
> ism; then to proclaim our constitution and expel the French empire
> from our soil; later when the people rebelled against Porfirio Díaz's
> dictatorship, which denied us the just application of the reform
> laws, and leaders like Villa and Zapata emerged, poor men just like
> us who have been denied the most elemental preparation so they
> can use us as cannon fodder and pillage the wealth of our country.
> They don't care that we have nothing, absolutely nothing, not even
> a roof over our heads, no land, no work, no health care, no food
> or education, not the right to freely and democratically elect our
> political representatives, nor independence from foreigners. There
> is no peace or justice for ourselves and our children.
>
> But today we say: ENOUGH IS ENOUGH! (EZLN 2001a: 13)

Through this assertion the Zapatistas situate themselves
squarely within both a national and a historical context as a rebel
response to the injustice of the existing political regime. This
notion of the justice and legitimacy of the Zapatista uprising is
echoed later in the declaration, as the EZLN invokes Article 39 of
the Mexican Constitution, which states that 'National Sovereignty
essentially and originally resides in the people. All political power
emanates from the people and its purpose is to help the people.
The people have, at all times, the inalienable right to alter or
modify their form of government' (EZLN 2001a: 14). Thus, the
uprising is located specifically and explicitly within the context

of a higher justice that has been denied to the Mexican people as a result of the ruling political powers.

While the central purpose of the 'First Declaration of the Lacandón Jungle' is ostensibly to declare war and to establish the EZLN's legitimacy as the true heir to revolutionary struggle in Mexico, it is important to be specific about who the EZLN is declaring war against. Significantly, the EZLN is careful throughout the declaration to distinguish who they perceive as their adversary. Specifically, the Zapatistas identify both the 'Mexican federal army, the pillar of the Mexican dictatorship from which we suffer', and the 'one-party system … led by Carlos Salinas de Gortari, the maximum and illegitimate federal executive that today holds power', as the targets of their hostilities (EZLN 2001a: 14). Following the uprising, it became commonplace for observers of various stripes to suggest that the Zapatistas declared war against the Mexican state, but this is most clearly not the case. The Zapatistas were very careful to identify those elements of the ruling regime they saw as being primarily responsible for the suffering of the Mexican people. Reinforcing this point, and in describing themselves and their cause, the EZLN states that

> We have the Mexican people on our side, we have the nation and the beloved tri-colored flag, highly respected by our insurgent fighters; our uniforms are black and red, symbol of our working people on strike; and we will always carry our flag, emblazoned with the letters 'EZLN,' the Zapatista National Liberation Army, into combat.
>
> From the outset, we reject all intentions to disgrace our just cause, accusing us of being drug traffickers, drug guerrillas, thieves, or other names that might be used by our enemies. Our struggle adheres to the Constitution and is inspired by its call for justice and equality. (2001a: 14)

In this passage, the Zapatistas clearly identify themselves as insurgents engaged in a just struggle and explicitly reject all other

identifications. The assertion of an essential Mexican identity
is obvious here, as is the patriotism implied by the reference
to the venerated status of the 'tri-colored' (Mexican) flag. The
passage finishes with a reference to the Mexican Constitution
and an implicit accusation that the ruling political powers have
betrayed both it and the Mexican people. Taken as a whole, these
assertions and denials serve to place the EZLN firmly within the
space occupied not only by a higher justice and legitimacy, but
by one occupied by the Mexican people as well.

In concluding the 'First Declaration of the Lacandón Jungle',
the EZLN makes a final appeal to the Mexican people and,
perhaps most significantly, outlines their fundamental demands.
This approach of engaging directly with the Mexican population
and grounding this engagement by evoking the most fundamental
claims upon which the Zapatista struggle is based — along with
their inherent justness — is a strategy that would serve both to
profoundly appeal to and to galvanize Mexican social movements
in the years to come. The declaration concludes with this final
passage:

> To the people of Mexico:
> We — men and women, whole and free — are conscious that
> the war we have declared is a last — but just — resort. For many
> years, the dictators have been waging an undeclared genocidal war
> against our people. Therefore, we ask for your decided participation
> to support this plan by the Mexican people who struggle for work,
> land, housing, food, health care, education, independence, freedom,
> democracy, justice, and peace. We declare that we will not stop
> fighting until the basic demands of our people have been met, by
> forming a government for our country that is free and democratic.
> (EZLN 2001a: 15)

There are several fundamental aspects of this final passage that
merit closer attention for what they indicate about Zapatismo and

its appeal as rebel political philosophy and practice. First, the passage expresses the Zapatistas' desire to participate with the Mexican people in 'forming a government for our country that is free and democratic'. This serves to illuminate the inclusive nature of the Zapatista project in that they openly solicit the participation of the rest of the population. It is of note that this participation is not necessarily rooted in armed insurrection. The mode of participation seems open to interpretation, and this is certainly something which would have a deep impact upon the way a diversity of other actors would respond to Zapatismo both nationally and transnationally. Perhaps most importantly, the stated desire in this passage is not the seizure of power, the toppling of the state, or even the implementation of a socialist programme; rather, it is the formation of 'a government that is free and democratic'. While some observers have suggested that Marcos and other Zapatista leaders would have seized power if they could have (see Oppenheimer 2002), the tone and explicit content of this declaration indicate the contrary. There is no agenda here that indicates any desire on the part of the Zapatistas to seize power or to implement their own regime. Quite simply, the Zapatistas call for a democratic opening in Mexico that will allow for the most basic needs, not only of the indigenous peoples but of the Mexican people in general, to be met. Rather than proposing a set project, the 'First Declaration of the Lacandón Jungle' is as much a call to participation and engagement as it is a call to arms. It is an invitation in the sense that it solicits the support and involvement of the Mexican people rather than assuming a leadership role for the EZLN itself, and in doing so it sets the stage for the radically democratic and emancipatory visions that would follow.

In the first clear indication of the Zapatista rebellion's significance within Mexico, Mexican civil society did indeed respond to the Zapatista call to action. With no direct ties to the EZLN, a mere twelve days after the Zapatista uprising began, Mexican civil society mobilized to demand an end to the war in Chiapas. The force of these national mobilizations compelled the Salinas government to declare a unilateral ceasefire in spite of the Mexican military's clear advantage. They also ushered in a new political moment in Mexico, one in which Mexican civil society would emerge as a powerful — albeit unpredictable — force alongside Zapatismo.

'Our sovereignty resides in civil society': The Second Declaration of the Lacandón Jungle

In the time between the issuing of the first and second declarations of the Lacandón Jungle the shooting war between the EZLN and the Mexican military had been brought to a tense halt twelve days after it began, as a result of the Mexican government's unilateral declaration of a ceasefire in the face of massive mobilizations across Mexico. In the time between these two declarations, the Mexican government had also entered into negotiations with the EZLN, mediated by Bishop Samuel Ruiz García (Muñoz Ramírez 2008: 117). The negotiations in the Cathedral of San Cristóbal de las Casas from 20 February until 2 March 1994 provided an excellent opportunity for members of the Zapatista leadership to begin what would become an enduring dialogue with national and international civil society (117). While the negotiations resulted in a document containing thirty-four government commitments and the leadership of the EZLN agreed to take it back to the communities, the communities ultimately resoundingly rejected it (118–19). In this context, the Zapatistas reaffirmed their commitment to maintaining the ceasefire while opening up a wider dialogue with civil society. The 'Second Declaration of the Lacandón Jungle' was issued on 12 June 1994 and represents the Zapatistas' attempt to reinvigorate the insurrectionary — though not necessarily armed or violent — and constitutive power of Mexican 'civil society' in pursuit of radical social transformation.

In many ways, the 'Second Declaration of the Lacandón Jungle' represents a considerable departure from the Zapatistas' declaration of war. Absent from this declaration is the rather bureaucratic and rigid style of the first declaration, replaced by significant literary flair and a powerful rhetorical argument, a mark of Marcos's increasing importance as a conduit for the Zapatistas' communication with the wider world. Invocations of dignity, resistance, hope and reason are woven throughout the declaration, articulating a terrain of struggle that exists beyond the merely material. Perhaps even more importantly, it is in this declaration that the concept of 'civil society' as it relates to the Zapatista movement emerges. The concept first appears in this document as the Clandestine Indigenous Revolutionary Committee outlines the events which have transpired since the first day of January 1994:

> The powers in Mexico ignored our just demand and permitted a massacre. However, this massacre only lasted twelve days. Another force, a force superior to any political or military power, imposed its will on the parties involved in the conflict. Civil society assumed the duty of preserving our country. It showed its disapproval of the massacre, and it obliged us to hold a dialogue with the government. (EZLN 2001d: 44)

It should be noted that not only does the concept of 'civil society' first appear in this declaration but the declaration itself is in fact directed to those who constitute it. The Zapatistas identify 'civil society' as 'our brothers and sisters in different nongovernmental organizations, in campesino and indigenous organizations, workers in the cities and in the countryside, teachers and students, housewives and squatters, artists and intellectuals, members of independent political parties, Mexicans' (48). The call made to this diverse group of people is the promise of the EZLN to maintain the ceasefire 'in order to permit civil society to organize in whatever forms they consider pertinent toward the goal of achieving a transition to democracy in our country' (44). While the claim may be made that the EZLN was in no position to mount any significant military operation against the Mexican army or the government even if it had wanted to, this assertion is nonetheless extremely important once one considers that it essentially entails the subordination of the armed insurgency to the civilian population of the Mexican nation. Thus, the transition from the first declaration to the second is already quite apparent. Rather than overcoming the army and overthrowing the executive branch of the federal government, the EZLN here affirms its role as a catalyst, but refers to civil society as the primary and only legitimate agent of change in Mexico. In the name of 'democracy, freedom, and justice' and in order to bring about the end of the 'state-party system', a reference to the PRI regime, civil society is asked to take the initiative and mobilize peacefully in order to achieve social change.

Another important concept which would become central to the Zapatista movement also emerges in the 'Second Declaration of the Lacandón Jungle': 'free and democratic space for political struggle' (EZLN 2001d: 46). This notion of 'political space' is a powerful concept, one that would become one of the most important themes of the Zapatista movement in the years to follow. As the declaration states:

> We aren't proposing a new world, but something preceding a new world: an antechamber looking into the new Mexico. In this sense, this revolution will not end in a new class, faction of a class, or group in power. It will end in a free and democratic space for political

struggle born above the fetid cadaver of the state-party system and the tradition of fixed presidential successions. (46)

Rather than a fixed political strategy or programme, the CCRI instead proposes a possibility, an opening, an 'antechamber' that provides the space both politically and socially for the Mexican people to be able freely and democratically to determine their future. As Marcos would later say, 'war should only be to open up space in the political arena so that the people can really have a choice.... We want to create the political space, and we want the people to have the education and the political maturity to make good choices' (Benjamin 1995: 61). Thus, in an environment characterized by the monopolization of power and authority by a select few, the Zapatistas' goal is to agitate for the formation of a space which would allow for choice and responsibility to be returned to the citizens of the Mexican nation themselves.

So how will this 'space' be realized and what does it entail? In the 'Second Declaration of the Lacandón Jungle', the EZLN extends an invitation to 'civil society' to participate in a 'National Democratic Convention' (CND) (EZLN 2001d: 49). The Zapatistas describe their vision of the convention as follows:

we call for a sovereign and revolutionary National Democratic Convention from which will come a transitional government and a new national law, a new constitution that will guarantee the legal fulfillment of the people's will.

This sovereign revolutionary convention will be national in that all states of the federation will be represented. It will be plural in that all patriotic sectors will be represented. It will be democratic in that it will make decisions through national *consultas*.

The convention will be presided over, freely and voluntarily, by civilians, prestigious public figures, regardless of their political affiliation, race, religion, sex, or age. (49)

The CND, described here in a largely abstract manner, is proposed by the Zapatistas as a way to pry open the political space in Mexico to move forward towards meaningful change without returning to the path of armed struggle. In the midst of a presidential campaign, and in an attempt to move from the abstract to the concrete, the National Democratic Convention was convoked in Zapatista territory from 5 August to 9 August 1994 (Muñoz Ramírez 2008: 120).

To make it a reality, 600 Zapatista troops worked under the direction of Comandante Tacho, the leader of the EZLN's Tojolabal zone, to construct the 'Aguascalientes', a meeting place in the jungles of Chiapas east of the Zapatista village of Guadalupe Tepeyac (Ross 2000: 73). Named for the town where the Constitutionalists, Villistas and Zapatistas had met during the Mexican Revolution in order to work out a post-revolutionary pact, the Aguascalientes consisted of a theatre seating 6,000, four inns, cookhouses, toilets and even a library (75). Subcomandante Marcos wrote letters of invitation to a diverse array of notable figures including: Mexican cultural critic Carlos Monsiváis; the famous Uruguayan writer Eduardo Galeano; Rigoberta Menchú, Mayan activist and Nobel Peace Prize recipient; radical US intellectual Noam Chomsky; Palestinian Liberation Organization leader Yasser Arafat; and African National Congress leader Nelson Mandela (73). While only a few of these high-profile figures attended, the message sent by the Zapatistas was clear: this revolutionary struggle went far beyond the borders of the 'conflict zone' in Chiapas.

The CND convened in San Cristóbal de las Casas on 6 August 1994, drawing approximately 7,000 diverse delegates from Mexican civil society, who divided into working groups focusing on specific themes: the 'transition to democracy', the 'inviability of the State–party', 'non-violent ways to democracy', 'elections, civil resistance, and defense of the will of the people', and 'formulation of a national project' (Womack 1999: 280). The next day CND delegates travelled into Zapatista territory to continue the Convention at the Aguascalientes (280).

When the CND concluded, no new constitution had been written and no government of transition had been formed, but CND attendants had agreed to work to dissolve the current political order — essentially, seven decades of one-party rule in Mexico — and to support the presidential candidate who professed support for the CND and its principles. Cuahtémoc Cárdenas, grandson of one of the most popular post-revolutionary presidents and leader of the Democratic Revolution Party (PRD), would be the candidate to take up the CND's cause. In spite of this challenge, the election yielded a clear victory for PRI candidate Ernesto Zedillo, with Cárdenas a distant third (Ross 2000: 78). A week after the election, Cárdenas publicly committed to not protesting the results of the election and asked his supporters to do the same, essentially abandoning the CND's struggle. While the Zapatistas had not expected Cárdenas to win the election, they had counted on a repeat performance of the massive electoral fraud the PRI had resorted to in the past in order to maintain power. If fraud did influence the election results, the evidence for it was not at all obvious. In the absence of this, the popular mobilizations against the current order hoped for by the CND and Zapatistas alike did not materialize (79). The PRI regime remained intact. Despite the PRI presidential victory and the significant blow dealt to the CND, the Zapatistas had proven that they could galvanize Mexicans outside the political system to mobilize in creative, non-state, non-traditional ways. Where this energy could take a larger movement and what political alternatives it offered were now the questions in need of answers.

'Our struggle is national':
The Third Declaration of the Lacandón Jungle

On the one year anniversary of the Zapatista uprising, the EZLN issued a new declaration. Following on the heels of the federal PRI victory bringing Ernesto Zedillo to the presidency, the Zapatistas issued their 'Third Declaration of the Lacandón Jungle' in response to what they saw as the failure of electoral politics to bring about meaningful change in the Mexican nation (EZLN 2004c). In many ways, this third declaration is an extension of themes that animated the declaration which preceded it. However, rather than calling for another National Democratic Convention, this declaration instead appeals to 'all social and political forces of the country, to all honest Mexicans, to all those who struggle for the democratization of the national reality' — in essence, to Mexican civil society — 'to form a National Liberation Movement' (MLN) (658). As the Zapatistas outline, the purpose of this movement is to 'struggle from a common accord, by all means, at all levels, for the installation of a transitional government, a new constitutional body, a new constitution, and the destruction of the system of the Party–State' (658). The thrust of this declaration remains very much the same as that of the previous one in that its aim is to generate a broad social front of opposition to the existing political regime — this time led by Democratic Revolution Party leader Cuahtémoc Cárdenas (658).

The context and reception of this declaration are essential to understanding its significance. With the new PRI government of Ernesto Zedillo installed in the halls of power and Cárdenas and the CND either unwilling or unable to mount a civil insurgency to complement their own, the Zapatistas were looking for a way to provoke civil society into action. In Chiapas, the race for governor had been won by the PRI candidate, Eduardo Robledo, over his pro-Zapatista challenger, Amado Avedaño (Womack 1999: 288). Unlike the presidential elections, however, in Chiapas allegations of electoral fraud were quickly followed by a campaign of civil unrest to block the PRI victory and to install Avedaño as governor (288). On 8 October 1994, in an effort to galvanize a national movement to match the one in Chiapas, the Zapatistas announced that they would no longer negotiate with the government, that they had mined roads into their territory, and that they had installed anti-aircraft units (288).

Following on the heels of this announcement, the State Democratic Assembly of the Chiapan People, a coalition of 180 organizations, declared a civil insurgency involving the formation of transitional governments in nine 'autonomous multi-ethnic' areas, which federal and state officials could not enter and where residents would not 'pay taxes, utility bills, or debts on federal, state, or municipal loans until Avedaño took office' (288–9). Because of the inability of the CND to generate a parallel movement on the national level to the one occurring in Chiapas, however, the Zedillo administration was not similarly threatened. More than this, Zedillo's interior minister, Esteban Moctezuma, was able to work out a deal with Avedaño that would allow Robledo to take the governorship while Avedaño would be allowed to run a 'government-in-rebellion' over the nine autonomous districts from offices in San Cristóbal (Ross 2000: 91). Avedaño accepted the deal but the Zapatistas had other plans.

On 11 December 1994, after publishing orders for its troops to engage in 'military missions', the EZLN announced the formation of nine new autonomous municipalities in the canyons of Chiapas (Womack, Jr 1999, 290). Then, at a press conference held at the Aguascalientes at 3.30 in the morning on 19 December, Subcomandante Marcos announced that two Zapatista units had penetrated federal army lines and established military positions in thirty-eight municipalities in the east of Chiapas, approximately half the state, and would recognize only Amado Avedaño as their governor (Ross 2000: 94). Welcomed by villagers, the Zapatista troops vanished before Mexican army units could reach them, leaving newly autonomous municipalities in their wake (95).

To top off this political nightmare for Zedillo and his government, after a poorly managed peso devaluation aimed at avoiding a full-blown economic crisis in the face of a $28 billion (USD) balance-of-payments deficit, Mexico's economy did collapse, prompting a huge bailout loan from the Clinton White House in the United States (97). In the face of this political and economic turmoil, the EZLN declared a truce and called for a new round of negotiations. On the first day of the truce, 1 January 1995, the EZLN issued the 'Third Declaration of the Lacandón Jungle'.

Two particular aspects of this declaration are of note. First, while the first two Zapatista declarations avoided referring in explicit terms to the fundamentally indigenous nature of the EZLN and its struggle, in the third declaration the EZLN names their uprising as 'the indigenous rebellion in Chiapas', as well as stating that the intent of this uprising was to 'call attention anew to the grave conditions of Mexican indigenous life' (EZLN 2004c: 656). In addition to the explicit indigenous identity invoked by this declaration, there is also a clear nationalist dimension to it. In this document, the Zapatistas refer to an internal coup within the ruling Institutional Revolutionary Party just prior to the federal elections which saw the chosen successor to the presidency assassinated, an event that the EZLN characterizes in the following manner:

> The [Institutional Revolutionary Party], the political arm of organized crime and drug traffickers, went into its most acute phase of decomposition, by resorting to assassination as the method of solving

its internal conflicts. Incapable of a civilized dialogue within its own party, the PRI bloodied the national soil. The shame of seeing the national colors usurped by the emblem of the PRI continues for all Mexicans. (EZLN 2004c: 656)

The Zapatistas further declare the 'Mexican flag, the justice system of the Nation, the Mexican Hymn, and the National Emblem' to be under the protection of the 'resistance forces' and removed from the use of the federal government until 'legality, legitimacy and sovereignty are restored to all of the national territory' (EZLN 2004c: 658). Even as they call for the overthrow of the president, the EZLN is extremely careful to situate itself as one of the true caretakers of the nation, as opposed to the 'grand gentlemen of power' who only seek to exploit the Mexican nation, its people and its resources for their own ends. As rebels, the Zapatistas situate themselves as the authentic defenders of the nation while the powerful are those who would destroy it. Given the cynicism, hostility and suspicion with which so many Mexicans had come to regard their government (see Chapter 1), the Zapatistas' reclamation of this tradition and its symbols reverberated powerfully.

Another theme strongly echoed in the third declaration is the notion of 'civil society'. However, in this declaration, 'civil society' is never referred to explicitly; rather, the EZLN approaches the concept from a different angle. In making their call for a National Liberation Movement, the Zapatistas appeal not to 'civil society' but to specific groups of the Mexican nation:

> We call upon the workers of the Republic, the workers in the countryside and the cities, the neighbourhood residents, the teachers and the students of Mexico, the women of Mexico, the young people of the whole country, the honest artists and intellectuals, the responsible religious members, the community-based militants of the different political organizations, to take up the means and forms

of struggle that they consider possible and necessary, to struggle for
the end of the Party–State system, incorporating themselves into the
National Democratic Convention if they do not belong to a party,
and to the National Liberation Movement if they are active in any of
the political opposition forces. (EZLN 2004c: 658)

While this passage bears stylistic resemblance to a similar
passage in the second declaration, the absence of the term 'civil
society' is noteworthy. As historian John Womack, Jr notes in his
evaluation of this declaration, the probable reason for this is that,
despite the best efforts of the Zapatistas, 'civil society' had failed
to mobilize effectively following the initial National Democratic
Convention (1999: 290). The MLN, so the Zapatistas hoped, was
the way beyond this inertia at the national level.

Perhaps as a result of this inaction, the EZLN in their third
declaration chose to call on specific actors to engage in diverse
actions in order to bring about the fall of the 'state–party' system
and implement a transitional government. Having said this, it
is essential to realize that while 'civil society' does not appear
as the single most important concept in this declaration, the
Zapatistas nevertheless acknowledge the fundamental importance
of diverse social actors in this struggle for national change. In
fact, the absence of the term itself may indeed refer us to a certain
problematization of the notion itself, in much the same way that
this notion is grappled with due to its amorphous nature by
contemporary theorists of democratic politics. By calling out
to diverse groups of Mexican citizens to engage in civil action
rather than calling out to 'civil society' itself, the Zapatistas may
be pointing directly to the need for these groups to form this
'civil society' themselves. Rather than assuming the existence
of such an entity as 'civil society', the 'Third Declaration of
the Lacandón Jungle' instead seeks to provoke the formation of
such a relationship. The responsibility for the realization of 'civil

society' is ultimately left in the hands of those whom it would comprise.

With economic crisis gripping the country and more Mexicans crushed by debt and socio-economic insecurity, the MLN was conceived, in part, as a vehicle to reach other sectors of society and to forge a front of struggle above class lines (Ross 2000: 102). The third National Democratic Convention was convoked in the city of Querétaro, 3–5 February 1995, and drew 4,000 delegates to discuss the MLN. No agreement could be reached about the MLN, and Cárdenas's leadership was ridiculed by the more radical delegates. The CND also dissolved at the MLN meetings, splintering into different groups that would never meet again as a single body. The Zapatistas had tried to galvanize Mexican civil society into taking novel political action in an effort to transform Mexico at the national level. In the incarnations of the CND and the MLN the effort had failed, but the political energy animating these Zapatista initiatives would find other possibilities to inhabit.

'The Zapatista Front of National Liberation': The Fourth Declaration of the Lacandón Jungle

On the second anniversary of the Zapatista uprising, the general command of the EZLN released the 'Fourth Declaration of the Lacandón Jungle'. Historically, this declaration came at a particularly interesting time for the Zapatista movement in terms of its public currency, and the EZLN most clearly sought to take advantage of this. In early 1995, Zedillo's administration had nearly followed the Mexican peso's precipitous descent. In an attempt to revive its tarnished image, the government sought to achieve a display of competence — in flagrant violation of the ceasefire — by releasing the identities of the Zapatista command to the public and simultaneously issuing arrest warrants for their capture (Womack 1999: 295). While the government held a press conference on 9 February 1995, to issue the warrants and, amongst other things, to 'unmask' Subcomandante Marcos as Rafael Sebastián Guillén Vicente (see Introduction), the Mexican army was invading Zapatista territory. Some 25,000 soldiers advanced into Zapatista territory in rebellion, intent on dismantling the autonomous municipalities and capturing — or killing — the Zapatista leadership, especially Subcomandante Insurgente Marcos (295).

The Zapatista leadership retreated in the face of the assault, dividing into smaller groups and aiming to regroup in the Montes Azules biosphere, a UNESCO ecological reserve that would prove exceptionally challenging for their pursuers (Ross 2000: 105). As the Zapatista *comandancia* fled, the brunt of the Mexican army's force was borne by the civilian residents of the area. As the army advanced it destroyed homes; stole goods, livestock and tools; damaged infrastructure; destroyed personal belongings; and drove entire communities into the mountains, where they were exposed to the elements, hunger and disease (Muñoz Ramírez 2008: 127). John Ross describes the situation in vivid detail:

> The soldiers were pissed off, frustrated by the fleeing villagers and the jungle heat. The few Indians that ventured out on the roads were grabbed for 'questioning' ... A score were beaten and jailed. In the empty villages, the soldiers rampaged through the flimsy little houses, pissing in the grain, shitting on the floor, and looting what little there was of value. In Pardo, they poisoned the corn and slashed the necks of the chickens. 'We want Marcos dead or alive!' they spray-painted on the ejido house, an allusion to the village's most celebrated resident. (2000: 107)

The result of this 'decisive action', however, was far from what the Zedillo government had hoped. Rather than crushing the movement, it reinvigorated it and brought elements of both Mexican and international 'civil society' into the picture once more (Womack 1999: 295). Indeed, in the words of John Womack, Jr, as national and international demonstrations brought an end to the government's illegal actions, Zedillo's attempt at demonstrating his authority made 'Marcos an international pop idol and the Indians of Chiapas globally famous and fantastically attractive' (295). With his credibility in tatters, Zedillo's only path out was to entreat the Zapatistas to participate in negotiations once more.

The Comisión de Concordia y Pacificación (COCOPA, the Commission of Concordance and Pacification) was the legislative commission charged with formulating a new law to facilitate dialogue between the EZLN and the federal government (Ross 2000: 116). Made of up representatives from the five political parties who held seats in Congress, with a rotating chairperson, COCOPA's law cleared Congress on 11 March 1995, and gave the EZLN thirty days to restart dialogue or the arrest warrants for Marcos and the other Zapatista leaders would be renewed (116). The EZLN proposed several sites in Mexico City for the peace talks but the federal government baulked — negotiations would have to be confined to Chiapas to keep the Zapatistas' claims limited to 'indigenous issues' (119). With the clock ticking towards the deadline, the two sides agreed to meet at the San Miguel *ejido* at the mouth of the Ocosingo canyon on 9 April (119–20). Due to the bounty on his head, Subcomandante Marcos would not attend the talks, leaving the stage to other indigenous Zapatista leaders (120). All told, there would be four parties attending the talks: the Zapatistas; the federal government; COCOPA; and the National Commission of Intermediation (CONAI), a mediation body formed by Bishop Samuel Ruiz and the Diocese of San Cristóbal de las Casas (120). Only two items were on the agenda for the first meeting: a set of negotiation protocols designed by CONAI and the setting of a place and date for the start of the real talks (120). After a day of tension, acrimony and distrust, an agreement was reached to begin negotiations on 20 April in the township of San Andrés Sacamch'en de los Pobres in the highlands of Chiapas.

The Dialogue for Peace and Reconciliation in Chiapas, as the peace talks were formally called, would continue, off and on, well into 1996. With the Mexican army present for 'security' purposes, Zapatista supporters crowded the town to provide a security cordon of their own for the comandantes. All told, the talks were supposed to involve six key thematic areas: (1) indigenous rights and culture; (2) democracy and justice; (3) well-being and development; (4) conciliation in Chiapas; (5) women's rights in Chiapas; and (6) end of hostilities (Muñoz Ramírez 2008: 129; see also Womack 1999: 297). Ultimately, accords would only be reached on the first thematic area — indigenous rights and culture — before negotiations broke off, and even they would require protracted struggle in order to be ratified and implemented by the Mexican government.

In August 1995, a National and International Consultation for Peace and Democracy was held throughout Mexico and online around the world (Muñoz Ramírez 2008: 129). The Consultation was called for by the Zapatistas and carried out by the election watchdog group Alianza Cívica (Civic Alliance) after what was left of the CND proved unable to take on the task (Womack 1999: 297). From 23 to 27 August, at 8,000 polling stations scattered across every state, 40,000 volunteers collected 1.2 million ballots (297). The Consultation asked six key questions: (1) 'Did the respondent support the EZLN's eleven demands (Democracy, Justice, Housing, et al.)?'; (2) 'Should the democratic forces in the country work together to achieve these demands?'; (3) 'Did

the Mexican state require a profound reform to achieve democracy?'; (4) 'Should the Zapatista Army of National Liberation
transform itself into a political force?'; (5) 'Should the Zapatista
Army of National Liberation join with other democratic forces to
form a new opposition alliance?'; (6) Should 'women ... be integrated on an equal basis into the nation's developing democratic
culture'? (Ross 2000: 136). The results of the Consultation were
overwhelming: 98 per cent supported the Zapatistas' demands; 92
per cent supported the formation of a broad front of opposition;
95 per cent supported reform to achieve a genuine democracy; 57
per cent supported the EZLN's transformation into an independent political force; 43 per cent supported the EZLN's joining
with other democratic forces; and 90 per cent supported the
equity of women (Womack 1999: 297). Internationally, nearly
100,000 votes were cast electronically from participants in fifty
countries, mirroring to a large extent the percentages the national
Consultation yielded (Muñoz Ramírez 2008: 129). While the scale
of participation and its international dimensions deeply troubled
the government, the idea of the Zapatistas becoming a more
conventional political force was deeply attractive. Even though the
Zapatistas were clear that they were not about to lay down their
arms, the federal government selectively interpreted the results
of the Consultation to suggest that this is what 'civil society'
wanted (Ross 2000: 138). The Zapatistas did not lay down their
arms; nor did they simply join the mainstream political system.
The Consultation had been a validation for the Zapatistas and
the peace talks continued — albeit with difficulty — with the
government.

As the San Andrés negotiations proceeded, the Zapatistas
broadened their demands while the Mexican government repeatedly attempted to regionalize and localize the scope of the talks
— a theme that had persisted throughout the rebellion. In this

context, the Zapatistas sought to encourage greater engagement
from Mexican civil society, issuing the call for an Intercontinental
Encuentro for Humanity and Against Neoliberalism to be held in
the jungles of Chiapas (see Chapter 4), and subverting the rigid
power dynamics of the negotiation table by inviting more than one
hundred advisers to join them because, so argued the Zapatistas,
there ought to be other voices represented at a dialogue about
national politics. The advisers included indigenous leaders, an-
thropologists, historians, intellectuals, as well as representatives of
diverse social and political organizations. In the midst of this, and
as 1995 entered its final months, the Zapatistas announced that
they were building four new 'Aguascalientes' — meeting places
between civil society and the Zapatistas — in the Selva, Norte
and Los Altos regions of Chiapas (Muñoz Ramírez 2008: 130).
The government interpreted this as a hostile move and the San
Andrés talks teetered precariously as the federal army intensified
its patrols and Subcomandante Marcos warned of the 'shadow
of war' (Womack 1999: 298). Nevertheless, the talks continued
and managed to produce a substantial working document on
indigenous rights that would be the basis for a 'Forum on Indian
Rights and Culture' to be held in San Cristóbal on 3–8 January
1996, to which representatives of Mexico's indigenous peoples
would be invited (Ross 2000: 150). The Zapatistas had clearly
succeeded in galvanizing Mexican civil society, but the massive,
grassroots movement to change radically the fabric of the social,
economic and political in Mexico did not seem any closer. Both
the CND and the MLN had been failures, and while there had
been notable successes, in the absence of a national movement
to complement the Zapatistas' work in Chiapas, the government
could continue to regionalize and 'ethnify' the conflict. In an
atmosphere of cautious optimism, and in an attempt to catalyse a
broad civil front of resistance at the national level as negotiations

over indigenous rights and culture entered a crucial stage, the Clandestine Indigenous Revolutionary Committee–General Command of the EZLN issued the 'Fourth Declaration of the Lacandón Jungle'.

The fourth Zapatista declaration is a document which is remarkable in many ways with respect to the other three declarations. First, this declaration is marked by a stylistic flair for argument and poetics, which has been attributed specifically to the writing of Subcomandante Marcos rather than the CCRI–CG as a whole (see Womack 1999: 298). Second, the document is the most steeped in indigenous identity of any of those to date, invoking as it does not only the indigenous history of the Zapatista movement but naming explicitly each of the indigenous language groups in Mexico as participants in a protracted 'rebellion against injustice' (EZLN 2004b: 661). Third, this declaration signals a return to the theme animating the 'Second Declaration of the Lacandón Jungle' in that it both revisits and dramatically expands upon the notion of 'civil society'. While the declaration begins, in standard Zapatista fashion, with a brief review of the conflict up to the present date, it proceeds to describe several new initiatives advanced by the Zapatistas in response to the National and International Consultation for Peace and Democracy:

> An initiative for the international arena expresses itself in a call to carry out an intercontinental dialogue in opposition to neoliberalism. The other two initiatives are of a national character: the formation of civic committees of dialogue whose base is the discussion of the major national problems and which are the seeds of a non-partisan political force; and the construction of the new Aguascalientes as places for encounters between civil society and Zapatismo. (EZLN 2004b: 664)

Very concrete places and practices of dialogue are advanced in this declaration from the outset, setting the stage for the main thrust of the declaration itself. It is of considerable significance to note that since the first declaration, there is an increasing tendency within each Zapatista declaration to call for the active participation of both national and international 'civil society' to participate in the struggle for 'A plural, tolerant, inclusive, democratic, just, free and new society' (EZLN 2004b: 666). What was originally a call to arms progressively became a call to dialogue and interaction through which this 'new society' may begin to crystallize.

While the Zapatistas outline their current endeavours early in the fourth declaration, the true purpose of this document is not fully revealed until almost the end. It is at this point where the Zapatistas issue their third and most forceful call for the support of Mexican 'civil society' in forming a broad social front of opposition:

> we call upon all honest men and women to participate in the new national political force which is born today: THE ZAPATISTA FRONT OF NATIONAL LIBERATION (FZLN), a civic and peaceful organization, independent and democratic, Mexican and national, which will struggle for democracy, liberty and justice in Mexico. The Zapatista Front of National Liberation is born today and we invite the participation of the workers of the Republic, the workers in the field and in the city, the indigenous people, the squatters, the teachers and students, Mexican women, the youth in all the nation, honest artists and intellectuals, religious people who are accountable, all those Mexican citizens who do not want Power but democracy, liberty, and justice for ourselves and for our children. (EZLN 2004b: 667)

In the broadest sense possible, the Zapatistas call for all 'honest Mexican men and women' to join in dialogue and struggle to achieve 'democracy, liberty, and justice'. 'Civil society' thus does not refer to any specific group of people or any political or social formation per se; rather, it includes the 'Mexican people' in the widest sense and excludes only those who wish to achieve traditional political power or are otherwise tied to the existing system.

The Zapatista conception of 'civil society' is one which embraces all those who wish to join in the struggle for political and social change and who are not tied to the idea that electoral politics or the seizure of power are the only avenues by which to realize this. Rather than establishing a specific political formation or indicating a specific group of organizations or individuals as comprising 'civil society', the concept instead articulates a space and a relationship for those who choose to participate in it — for all those who want to build a 'world capable of holding many worlds'. Most significantly, this notion of 'civil society' is a space and a relationship that are voluntary, autonomous and democratic. In this conceptualization, 'civil society' has no particular form or agenda; rather, it is characterized by 'the autonomy of the organizations constituting civil society, their independence from the State and their antagonism towards it' (Esteva 1999: 158). Furthermore, it should be noted that while this formulation of 'civil society' may seem impossibly broad and amorphous, 'It is not constituted by masses: it is not a herd, but a multiplicity of diverse groups and organizations, formal or informal, of people who act together for a variety of purposes' (159). Thus, 'civil society' is a space of liberation and engagement for all those who wish to participate in it, and it is a space and a relationship given form and content only by those who take up the responsibility of constituting it. While this understanding of 'civil society' may seem extraordinarily undefined to some, it must be appreciated that this conceptualization in fact exemplifies the Zapatista notion of dialogue and engagement as it allows for and, in fact, necessitates multiplicity, difference and antagonism

as essential elements involved in the construction of a radically
plural and inclusive world.

The proposed structure of the Zapatista Front of National
Liberation is of particular interest in terms of what it tells us
about the way the Zapatistas envision the project of radical social
change. In the fourth declaration, the Zapatistas delve into considerable conceptual detail to express the relationship between
the EZLN and the members of Mexican civil society who wish to
struggle in common with them. The CCRI's — perhaps Marcos's
— prose is highly abstract and somewhat obscure if taken as a
blueprint or a concrete frame of reference by which to structure
a new social movement. However, if the content of this declaration is taken to be symbolic rather than literal, allusive instead
of programmatic, it becomes clear that what the Zapatistas are
describing is not a new structure or a new form of organization
but rather a reconfiguring of the manner in which people relate
to one another:

> We invite national [civil] society, those without a party, the citizen
> and social movement, all Mexicans to construct this new political
> force.
>
> A new political force which will be national. A new political force
> based in the EZLN.
>
> A new political force which forms part of a broad opposition
> movement, the National Liberation Movement, as a space for citizen
> political action where there may be a confluence with other political
> forces of the independent opposition, a space where popular wills
> may encounter and coordinate united actions with one another.
>
> A political force whose members do not exert nor aspire to hold
> elective positions or government offices in any of its levels. A politi-
> cal force which does not aspire to take power. A force which is not
> a political party.
>
> A political force which can organize the demands and proposals
> of those citizens and is willing to give direction through obedience.
> A political force which can organize a solution to the collective

problems without the intervention of political parties and of the government. We do not need permission in order to be free. The role of the government is the prerogative of society and it is its right to exert that function.

A political force which struggles against the concentration of wealth in the hands of a few and against the centralization of power. A political force whose members do not have any other privilege than the satisfaction of having fulfilled its commitment.

A political force with local, state and regional organization which grows from the base, which is its social force. A political force given birth by the civic committees of dialogue.

A political force which is called a FRONT because it incorporates organizational efforts which are non-partisan, and has many levels of participation and many forms of struggle.

A political force called ZAPATISTA because it is born with the hope and the indigenous heart which, together with the EZLN, descended again from the Mexican mountains.

A political force with a program of struggle with 13 points. Those contained in the First Declaration of the Lacandon Jungle and added throughout the past two years of insurgency. A political force which struggles against the State–Party system. A political force which struggles for a new constituency and a new constitution. A political force which does not struggle to take political power but for a democracy where those who govern, govern by obeying. (EZLN 2004b: 667–8)

The rebel vision of radical political possibility offered by the Zapatistas in this passage is one in which the concept of political 'space', radical democratic practice, and a highly egalitarian and autonomous structure are combined in order to generate the hope of achieving a new social order. Rather than being merely a tool for social change, the Zapatista Front of National Liberation is envisioned here as a place to begin living the kinds of relations a liberated and just society would be marked by. It is essential to note that the front which the Zapatistas are proposing is one based in the concepts of Zapatismo but which is by no means limited to them. The central notion here is that there must be a space for dialogue, difference and accord if exploitive structures are to give way to just, democratic and liberated ones. In this case, civil society is envisioned as a partner to the EZLN rather than an addition to it, and the EZLN, rather than being a vanguard, in fact operates more as the impetus and drive for this civil movement, 'the hope and indigenous heart which ... descended again from the Mexican mountains'.

The political atmosphere surrounding the Zapatista rebellion during this period was dynamic and charged. In early 1996, the EZLN convoked the Special National Forum on Indigenous Rights and Culture in San Cristóbal de las Casas, drawing more than 500 representatives from thirty-five different indigenous peoples in Mexico (Muñoz Ramírez 2008: 134). This forum resulted in the formation of the politically independent National Indigenous Congress, as well as yielding a consensus decision ratifying the EZLN's positions in the San Andrés talks and affirming that indigenous autonomy would be the basic principle upon which to build a new relationship between indigenous peoples and the Mexican state (134). In addition to this, at the end of January 1996, the Zapatistas issued the 'First Declaration of La Realidad for Humanity and Against Neoliberalism', calling for continental encounters to be held in preparation for an Intercontinental Encuentro for Humanity and Against Neoliberalism that would be hosted by the Zapatista base communities in rebel territory (135). Following on the heels of the Zapatistas' call to form the FZLN, the Zapatistas returned to the negotiating table with the government hoping to catalyse a critical mass of public support to push for a greatly expanded discussion on issues of social, political and economic transformation at a national level.

Peace talks continued on 10 January 1996 at San Andrés in the highlands of Chiapas. The Zedillo administration was eager to bring the talks to 'a praiseworthy end' — praiseworthy, at least, in a way it could sell publicly (Womack 1999: 307). As negotiations continued, the government defended the principle of 'national sovereignty' and refused to discuss any inclusion of 'autonomy' for indigenous peoples in the Constitution (307). Government negotiators also managed to separate issues of 'Indigenous Rights and Culture' from issues such as agrarian reform (307). But the government also made concessions, including ceding 'rights of jurisdiction' to indigenous municipalities and their recognition as 'entities of public law' (307–8). In practice, these concessions would devolve political power to indigenous municipalities, allowing them to make their own decisions about political organization within and between indigenous communities, as well as providing them with access to resources to engage in their own social development projects but all within the context of 'national unity' (313). While the Zapatista leadership wanted to press for more, they lacked the public pressure on a national level to push the government further (308). The Zapatista leadership consulted its own support bases over the accords and the results were telling: while the accords were deemed to be minimally acceptable, 96 per cent also protested their failure to address demands such as municipal and regional autonomy, agrarian reform, women's rights, subterranean resource rights, and the freeing of political prisoners (Womack 1999: 308; Ross 2000: 161). Despite the protest vote, negotiations concluded on 18 January 1996 with several accords, and on 16 February the EZLN and the Mexican government signed the accords, making them 'commitments' (Womack 1999: 308). While the Zedillo government wanted to use the accords as a public relations opportunity to convince the wider world that Mexico was now once again 'open for business', the Zapatista leadership refused to make the signing of the accords a public display, refusing even to be photographed in the act, a symbolic

gesture indicating their disappointment in the outcome of negotiations and their anticipation of future government deception (Ross
2000: 162–3). Internationally, the accords held the promise of
easing the stigma borne by the Zedillo administration for its
failure to address justly the underlying grievances animating the
Zapatista rebellion. Indeed, the Zapatistas' international supporters, particularly in North America and Western Europe, had
become a constant thorn in the side of the Zedillo government,
hounding the president and his officials on their trips outside of
Mexico. By not giving him his symbolic moment, the Zapatistas
effectively denied Zedillo the iconic image of a conflict resolved
he so longed for, even as they signed accords they did not fully
believe in. Their symbolic act of resistance anticipated a renewed
landscape of crisis and conflict on the horizon.

While the first accords were signed, ratification and implementation would be another matter entirely, and although the
peace process was now supposed to proceed to the other five
thematic discussions — the next a dialogue on 'Democracy and
Justice' — the Mexican government demonstrated utter indiffer-
ence to proceeding any further on matters that moved beyond
regional or indigenous issues (Muñoz Ramírez 2008: 140). In
the Chiapas countryside, Zedillo's government was working to
end the land occupations by campesinos that had proliferated
since the uprising through a combination of land distribution to
some, compensation to wealthy landowners, and repression of
those land reclaimers who could not be bought out (Ross 2000:
165–6). At the same time, a steady stream of celebrities descended
on Zapatista territory during the spring and summer of 1996 to
meet Marcos and the Zapatistas, including Hollywood director
Oliver Stone; actor Edward James Olmos; former guerrilla Régis
Debray; Danielle Mitterrand, former first lady of France; and the
renowned human rights activists from Argentina, the Mothers of

the Plaza de Mayo (167–8). Marcos met with them all, drawing a media circus into rebel territory in Chiapas in the process and doing so in order to allow Zapatista communities to begin to feed themselves again (168). Because of the military invasion in the spring of 1995, Zapatista communities had not had the chance to plant their crops properly. Now hunger was beginning to set in and another season of planting was in jeopardy due to the stifling presence of the Mexican military and their constant patrols and harassment. The presence of international celebrities offered an easing of the military's noose and afforded the communities a chance to plant (168). In the spring and summer of 1996, the Zapatistas would host two other high-profile events that would draw national and international supporters to Zapatista territory: the Continental Forum for Humanity and Against Neoliberalism and the Intercontinental Encuentro for Humanity and Against Neoliberalism. Seeking to connect with other struggles in other places that were confronting neoliberal capitalism and defending human dignity, the Zapatistas issued the 'First Declaration of La Realidad for Humanity and Against Neoliberalism':

The Zapatista Army of National Liberation Speaks...

To all who struggle for human values of democracy, liberty and justice.

To all who force themselves to resist the world crime known as 'Neoliberalism' and aim for humanity and hope to be better, be synonymous of future.

To all individuals, groups, collectives, movements, social, civic and political organizations, neighborhood associations, co-operatives, all the lefts known and to be known; non-governmental organizations, groups in solidarity with struggles of the world people, bands, tribes, intellectuals, indigenous people, students, musicians, workers, artists, teachers, peasants, cultural groups, youth movements, alternative communication media, ecologists, tenants, lesbians, homosexuals, feminists, pacifists.

> To all human beings without a home, without land, without work,
> without food, without health, without education, without freedom,
> without justice, without independence, without democracy, without
> peace, without tomorrow.
> To all who, with no matter to colors, race or borders, make of
> hope a weapon and a shield.
> And calls together to the First Intercontinental Gathering for Human-
> ity and Against Neoliberalism. (EZLN 1996)

In preparation for the Intercontinental Encuentro to be held from 27 July to 3 August 1996 in Zapatista territory in rebellion, the Zapatistas proposed continental planning meetings to be held in: Berlin, Germany (Europe); La Realidad, Mexico (Americas); Tokyo, Japan (Asia); an unspecified location in Africa; and Sydney, Australia (Oceania) (EZLN 1996). For the Zapatista struggle in Chiapas, the Continental Forum and the Intercontinental Encuentro also brought international attention to bear on Chiapas at a particularly delicate time for the movement. The two anti-neoliberal gatherings drew thousands of national and international supporters to rebel territory in 1996, providing a measure of security for Zaapatista communities, inspiring what would shortly become a global movement (see Chapter 4), and providing a space to learn about other struggles and to begin to build bridges between them.

While the Continental Forum and the Intercontinental Encuentro were great successes for the Zapatistas, the second round of dialogue with the government over the reform of the state was going less well. The government and the EZLN tabled two entirely different visions of the reforms necessary to build 'Justice and Democracy' in Mexico, the former limiting itself to marginal electoral reforms while the latter sought a radical transformation of the Constitution and a renegotiation of NAFTA (Ross 2000: 187). Negotiations never got off the ground, and as of 12 August 1996 both sides had walked away from the negotiating table in San Andrés and would not return (188). While the Zedillo government continued to militarize Chiapas and to arm and train paramilitary groups, the government also reneged on its promise to ratify the constitutional reforms based on the initial San Andrés Accords and drafted by COCOPA, dealing a critical blow to the peace process (Muñoz Ramírez 2008: 148).

In the face of these events, the EZLN responded to a request by the National Indigenous Congress to send a representative to its meeting in Mexico City, directly challenging the will of business and political elites who sought to bar the Zapatistas from travelling outside of Chiapas. Indeed, the Zedillo government warned that the Dialogue Law that had suspended the arrest warrants for the Zapatista leadership was contingent on the EZLN remaining limited to Chiapas — any attempt to travel outside the state would, in its view, constitute a violation of the law and render the Zapatistas legitimate targets of police and military action (Ross 2000: 198). As the government and the EZLN headed towards open confrontation, the COCOPA managed to broker an eleventh-hour deal that would allow ten Zapatistas to travel to Mexico City — unarmed but masked — so long as none of them had outstanding arrest warrants against them (199). The Zapatistas would deliver the master stroke in this political drama, however. Rather than sending a delegation of ten, the Zapatistas sent a single delegate: a tiny, critically ill Tzotzil woman, Comandanta Ramona. To reporters, Marcos explained that Ramona was dying and that it was her last wish to go to the National Indigenous Congress and to 'tell them what the EZLN is all about' (200). Of course, the trip to Mexico City was also an opportunity to get Ramona the medical care she so desperately needed as her kidneys had failed her (200). Journalist John Ross summarizes the significance of sending Ramona as the Zapatistas' delegate to the CNI:

Sending Ramona to the congress was a measure of the EZLN's in-
genuity. Not only did the move put them back on the front page, but
the image of this tiny, terminally ill Indian woman traveling alone up
to the capital when, for weeks, the *mal gobierno* [bad government]
had been painting the Zapatistas as war demons, handed the rebels
the moral high ground yet again. (2000: 200)

When Ramona arrived in Mexico City, she was greeted by
a multitude of activists who provided an unexpected security
cordon for the comandanta. On 12 October 1996, in commemoration of 504 years of indigenous resistance to colonialism and
genocide, Comandanta Ramona delivered a speech to a crowd
of 50,000 in the central plaza of Mexico City (201). Through
Ramona, the Zapatistas issued a rallying cry to Mexican civil
society and a warning to the powerful who sought to silence
them as Ramona invoked what would become a key slogan of the
Zapatista movement: 'never again a Mexico without us' (Muñoz
Ramírez 2008: 147).

In the weeks following her historic speech as the first contemporary Zapatista to take Mexico City, Ramona received a
kidney transplant through the fundraising efforts of the Zapatista
Front of National Liberation (Ross 2000: 201). Unfortunately,
the FZLN would not accomplish much more than this following
its calling into existence by the EZLN. While it has endured, it
had done so largely as 'a kind of Zapatista think tank, a network
of committees of electronic correspondence with some influence
in Mexico's southern states on local social legislation and policy'
(Womack 1999: 332). John Womack, Jr has postulated three
hypotheses as to why the FZLN also failed to live up to the
hopes the Zapatistas invested in it: (1) the US government wanted
a situation characterized by 'low-intensity warfare' in Mexico
because, historically speaking, it is precisely under conditions
of domestic crisis that the USA has got the most out of Mexico,

thus the US government had no interest in allowing the FZLN to evolve into a viable, unarmed political alternative to the Zapatista army; (2) the Mexican population simply ended up being much more conservative than the Zapatista leadership ever understood or appreciated and thus was unwilling to mobilize for radical change; (3) as the Mexican government eagerly anticipated the supplanting of the EZLN by the FZLN, the Zapatista leadership put the Front on hold (328–30). While the exact reason for the FZLN's marginality is not known, it became clear that the FZLN would not be the mechanism capable of generating a civil uprising to complement the Zapatistas. The Zapatistas had scored a moral victory and Ramona's life had been saved, but politically they continued to struggle to catalyse a popular movement beyond Chiapas that could begin to undertake a national project of radical social, economic and political transformation.

'This is the hour of national civil society': The Fifth Declaration of the Lacandón Jungle

The 'Fifth Declaration of the Lacandón Jungle' was issued by the General Command of the EZLN on 19 July 1998. This fifth declaration was issued at a very particular point in time, a period following the failure of the Mexican government to implement the San Andrés Accords on Indigenous Rights and Culture after they had been agreed upon through negotiations. It also followed on the heels of the Acteal massacre, in which forty-five Tzotzil Indians — mainly women and children — were murdered by pro-PRI paramilitaries with the full complicity of the Mexican armed forces and police.

In the fall of 1997, in the Los Altos region of Chiapas, the municipality of Chenalhó had become wracked by violence. In this municipality, two parallel authorities existed: the pro-PRI government ensconced in the county seat of San Pedro Chenalhó while the pro-Zapatista autonomous government was located in Polhó, 24 kilometres away (Ross 2000: 235). The existence of parallel authorities — one pro-government, the other pro-Zapatista — was not an unusual occurrence in Chiapas following the uprising. In Chenalhó, however, tensions had reached boiling point and erupted into open violence with houses burned to the ground and people murdered. Local police and military turned a blind eye to PRI-affiliated paramilitary groups beginning to arm themselves; in fact, there is considerable evidence to suggest government and military officials had a hand in facilitating the arming and training of these groups as well as providing them with considerable latitude to operate. Compounding this, the suspension of peace talks exacerbated what was already a dangerous and violent situation (Muñoz Ramírez 2008: 162). In Chenalhó, late 1997 brought widespread displacement of indigenous communities affiliated with or sympathetic to the Zapatista rebellion and the EZLN warned of a disaster in the making with thousands of refugees surrounded by paramilitaries, police and military units and the hired guns of wealthy landowners (162). While the government of Chiapas claimed to be bringing peace to Chenalhó — going so far as to buy full-page advertisements in national newspapers to announce this — paramilitary groups operated unchecked, terrorizing, looting and destroying rebel communities in the region (Ross 2000: 238). With Bishop Samuel Ruiz's CONAI mediation body warning of an impending atrocity along with the diocese's Fray Bartolomé Human Rights Centre and NGOs like Human Rights Watch echoing the call, state and national officials refused to act. The stage was set for the single worst atrocity committed during the course of the Zapatista rebellion.

The event occurred on 22 December 1997. Mexican journalist Gloria Muñoz Ramírez describes the events of this day when one of the most atrocious and sadly predictable massacres in the history of the [Mexican] nation occurred. In the community of Acteal, located in the township of Chenalhó in Los Altos of Chiapas, forty-five indigenous people, most children and women belonging to the civilian group 'Las Abejas' ['The Bees'] were massacred with firearms and machetes by sixty armed men from a paramilitary band made up of indigenous from the PRI and the Cardenist Front (PFCRN). In the attack another twenty-five persons were wounded, including several children. The shooting lasted over six hours, while dozens of Public Security police remained 200 meters away from where the killings took place, listening to the shots and screams without lifting a finger. (2008: 164)

The Abejas were not Zapatistas — indeed, they were explicitly pacifist — but they were sympathetic to the Zapatistas' cause, if not their armed path. The community was singled out as an object lesson to other rebels and because there were some allegations that members of the Acteal Abejas had participated in an ambush that killed a pro-government indigenous man (Ross 2000: 239). The massacre was premeditated, punitive, elaborately deliberate, and carried out with total impunity. The massacre at Acteal provoked hundreds of different protest actions throughout Mexico and around the world. Zedillo's government, ever inept and crude at engaging the Zapatista rebellion, had sunk to a new low in the eyes of the international community. While activists denounced the massacre and the government complicity that had facilitated it, so too did the government of the United States, the prime minister of France Lionel Jospin, Pope John Paul II, the European Union, the secretary of the Organization of American States, and the United Nations (Muñoz Ramírez 2008: 165). In the shadow of Acteal, the EZLN issued its fifth declaration.

The 'Fifth Declaration of the Lacandón Jungle' begins, as the other declarations do, with a brief synopsis of the events to date with regard to the Zapatista movement and the reaffirmation on the part of the EZLN that the struggle continues. Following this, the CCRI–CG of the EZLN calls 'all honest men and women to the struggle for the: "Recognition of the rights of Indian peoples and for an end to the war of extermination"' (EZLN 2004a: 678). In pursuit of this objective, the EZLN first calls upon the indigenous populations of Mexico to join in the struggle. Following this, the Zapatistas declare that 'It is the hour of National Civil Society and the independent political and social organizations' (678). Once again, the Zapatistas reach out to the people of Mexico who are not complicit in the existing system of exploitation and extermination. Specifically, the declaration characterizes this 'hour' as follows:

> It is the hour of the campesinos, of the workers, of the teachers, of the students, of the professionals, of the religious men and women, of the journalists, of the neighbours, of the small shopkeepers, of the debtors, of the artists, of the intellectuals, of the disabled, of the sero-positives, of the homosexuals, of the lesbians, of the men, of the women, of the children, of the young people, of the old persons, of the unions, of the cooperatives, of the campesino groups, of the political organizations, of the social organizations. (EZLN 2004a: 678–9)

Thus, once more, 'civil society' is referred to not in any exact or predetermined manner, but rather in the form of a broad spectrum of people who are unified only by their rebellion against a political, social, and economic system that exploits and degrades them all in some respect. The EZLN continues this appeal by stating:

> We call on them, together with the Indian peoples and with us, to struggle against the war and for the recognition of indigenous rights, for the transition to democracy, for an economic model which serves the people and does not serve itself, for a tolerant and inclusive society, for respect for difference, and for a new country where peace with justice and dignity will be for everyone. (EZLN 2004a: 679)

What is particularly significant about this passage is not its rhetorical similarity to the three preceding declarations but that the end of the war against indigenous peoples and the recognition of indigenous rights are not seen as the final step of the social change project stimulated by the Zapatista rebellion. Indeed, the Zapatistas affirm this quite plainly, stating that 'This is the hour of the struggle for the rights of the Indian peoples, as a step towards democracy, liberty and justice for all' (EZLN 2004a: 680). In this context, the Zapatistas call for a National Consultation on the constitutional reforms drafted by the Commission on Concordance and Pacification and 'for an end to the war of Extermination' (680).

An urgency and a clear sense of time animate the 'Fifth Declaration of the Lacandón Jungle'. In part, this sense comes from the General Command's repeated rhetorical invocation that it is 'the hour' of different actors to demand a recognition of indigenous rights and an end to the war. Beyond rhetoric, there is an immediacy to this declaration, one that is important to appreciate as a conscious strategy of Subcomandante Marcos and other Zapatista leaders to provoke renewed action on the part of Mexican civil society in pressing for the recognition of the constitutional reforms on indigenous rights and culture. In order to carry out this National Consultation, the Zapatistas held a meeting between the EZLN and civil society in San Cristóbal de las Casas on 20–22 November 1998 attended by thirty-two Zapatista delegates and more than 3,000 Mexicans from all over the country (Muñoz Ramírez 2008: 177–8). The meeting helped codify the four questions that would constitute the consultation called for by the fifth declaration — two which would address indigenous rights, one which would deal with the question of peaceful versus armed social change, and one which would address the question of the nature of the democratic process (178).

The Sixth Declaration of the Lacandón Jungle
and the Other Campaign

Seven years would elapse between the EZLN General Command's issuing of the fifth and sixth 'Declarations of the Lacandón Jungle'. Of course, the Zapatistas were far from quiescent during this period. In 2000, National Action Party candidate and former Coca-Cola executive Vicente Fox defeated the Institutional Revolutionary Party candidate Francisco Labastida in Mexico's presidential elections, ending more than seven decades of one-party rule in the country. Fox, former governor of the state of Guanajuato, rode his own maverick personal style — complete with cowboy boots, big moustache, silver belt buckle and straight talk — and what had become a powerful current within Mexican society for political change all the way to the presidency. The Zapatistas welcomed the victorious Fox in a press conference held in the Zapatista village of La Realidad on 2 December 2000 (Ross 2006: 40). Mayor Moisés, Comandante Tacho and Subcomandante Marcos greeted the new president with: 'We want to remind the Fox that he has inherited a war here in Mexico's southeast ... and he will not win it.... Mister Fox, you start at zero confidence and credibility with us' (40–41). Fox had famously claimed he could solve the conflict in Chiapas in fifteen minutes, but the Zapatistas had their own plans. While Fox was eager to restart the dialogue with the Zapatistas en route to 'pacifying' Chiapas, the Zapatistas were clear that no further talks would occur without the fulfilment of three key signals: (1) passage of the San Andrés Accords on Indigenous Rights and Culture into law; (2) the release of all Zapatista political prisoners; (3) a dismantling of the military bases closest to the five Zapatista Aguascalientes in Chiapas (40). In order to press for the passage of the San Andrés Accords, the Zapatistas announced that they would be sending a delegation to Mexico City to defend the Accords before the legislature. The Zapatistas were once again talking about taking Mexico City.

The Zapatista delegation would be made up of twenty-three indigenous leaders: Comandantes David, Tacho, Zebedeo, Susana, Javier, Yolanda, Isaias, Bulmaro, Abel, Moises, Esther, Maxo, Ismael, Eduardo, Gustavo, Sergio, Omar, Filemon, Abraham, Daniel, Mister, Fidelia and Alejandro (Subcomandante Marcos 2004b, 527). Accompanying the delegation would also be Subcomandante Marcos, but in its engagement with Congress it would be the indigenous comandantes who would take the lead. With hearings on the San Andrés Accords scheduled for a special session of Congress in March 2001, the Zapatistas announced they would arrive in the capital on 11 March after their caravan travelled a long, circuitous route through the Mexican Republic in order to raise public support for the passage of the Accords (Ross 2006: 41). For his part, Fox publicly welcomed the Zapatista caravan. Unarmed but masked, and with considerable fanfare, the Zapatista delegation left San Cristóbal de las Casas on 24 February 2001 (Muñoz Ramírez 2008: 212, 222). The route the Zapatista caravan followed would take them from Chiapas through the states of Oaxaca, Verecruz, Puebla, Hidalgo, Queretaro, Guanajuato, Michoácan, México, Morelos and Guerrero, arriving finally in Mexico City (Subcomandante Marcos 2004b, 528–31). In each state, the Zapatistas met with indigenous peoples, participated in rallies and other public events, and continued the Zapatista encounter with Mexican civil society.

The March of the People the Colour of Earth, or the March for Indigenous Dignity, was nothing short of historic in its significance. The circumstances are enough to understand why: in Mexico, a nation-state like so many others in the Americas plagued by a long history of racism and extreme violence toward indigenous peoples, a delegation of twenty-three indigenous leaders was advancing on the heart of Mexican political power to demand an audience with Congress and make the case for the recognition of indigenous rights, dignity and autonomy. Beyond this a rebel group was travelling unarmed — but not disarmed — through Mexico not to beg an audience with the powerful but to continue its long, complex engagement with that amorphous, diverse and unpredictable entity referred to as 'civil society' (see Monsiváis 2002). Marcos explained the significance of the march a few days before it began to Ignacio Ramonet, the Spanish journalist and writer and then editor-in-chief of *Le Monde Diplomatique*:

> This is not Marcos's march nor the EZLN's. It is the march of the poor, the march of all the Indian peoples. It's intended to show that the days of fear are over. Our aim is to get the Mexican Congress to recognize the identity of indigenous people as 'collective subjects' by right. Mexico's constitution doesn't recognize Indians. We want the government to accept that Mexico has a variety of peoples; that our indigenous peoples have their own political, social, and economic forms of organization; and that they have a strong connection to the land, to their communities, their roots, and their history.
>
> We are not asking for an autonomy that will exclude others. We are not calling for independence. We don't want to proclaim the birth of the Maya nation, or fragment the country into lots of small indigenous countries. We are just asking for the recognition of the rights of an important part of Mexican society which has its own forms of organization that it wants to be legally recognized.
>
> Our aim is peace. A peace based on a dialogue which is not a sham. A dialogue that will lay the groundwork for rebuilding Chiapas and make it possible for the EZLN to enter ordinary political life. Peace can only be had by recognizing the autonomy of the indigenous peoples. This recognition is an important precondition for the EZLN to end its clandestine existence, give up armed struggle, participate openly in regular politics and also fight the dangers of globalization. (Ramonet 2002: 133–4)

With millions of Mexicans following the Zapatista caravan and more waiting in the nation's capital for their arrival, the Zapatistas had firmly taken the political spotlight and used this to demand an audience with the Congress to press for the passage of the original Accords. Of course, the march was also an opportunity for the Zapatistas to revitalize ties with Mexican civil society as their route wound toward the centre of Mexican political power. When the Zapatista delegation arrived in Mexico City on 11 March, they were greeted by a crowd of 250,000 in the Zócalo. Delivering a powerful address to the gathered supporters, the Zapatista delegation announced:

> MEXICO CITY: We are here. We are here as the rebellious color of the earth which shouts:
>> Democracy!
>> Liberty!
>> Justice!
> Mexico: We did not come to tell you what to do, or to guide you along any path. We came in order to humbly, respectfully, ask you to help us. For you to not allow another day to dawn without this flag having an honorable place for we who are the color of the earth. (EZLN 2002: 114)

The Zapatistas had done what the EZLN could not do in January 1994: they had taken Mexico City without firing a single shot and, to the great consternation of Mexico's political class, they had rallied Mexicans — and supporters internationally — to demand fundamental respect for the dignity of indigenous peoples and their capacity for self-determination.

Encamped at the National Anthropology School, the Zapatistas were offered by Congress a meeting with twenty congressional leaders to discuss the indigenous rights bill (Ross 2002: 191). This was not what the delegation had trekked to Mexico City for and the offer was labelled 'humiliating' and flatly rejected (191).

The subcomandante and the comandantes waited a week for another offer from Congress, spending the time meeting with the tremendous diversity of people who came to see them and attending a massive rally in their honour at the National Autonomous University of Mexico (191). When no new offer was forthcoming, the Zapatista delegation announced it was leaving. Faced with being labelled a racist, elite political class that was unwilling to listen to indigenous peoples on the issue of indigenous rights, President Fox scrambled to offer the Zapatistas enticements to stay: a personal meeting between himself and Subcomandante Marcos; the closing of military bases in Zapatista territory; the release of more political prisoners (193). But the Zapatistas had not come for a photo op with Fox, they had come to address the Congress of the Mexican nation. On 22 March, the day Congress was set to begin debating whether or not to allow the Zapatistas to address them, the Zapatistas staged a farewell rally outside of Congress in front of 20,000 supporters, who were prepared to storm the Congress if they refused to allow the delegation in (193–4). The results of the debate came as a complete surprise to most: in a vote of 220 to 210, Congress voted to allow the Zapatista delegation in to address them (194).

When the Zapatista delegation finally gained access to the Congress on 28 March it was not Marcos but Comandanta Esther, an indigenous woman, who took the podium and delivered the Zapatistas' core message to the Mexican Congress (Muñoz Ramírez 2008: 224). Explaining Marcos's absence to the Congress, Esther explained, 'Marcos is a Subcomandante — that is, he works for us. We are the comandantes of the Zapatista Army of National Liberation and we speak for ourselves' (Ross 2006: 80). The Zapatista comandantes explained to the Congress the vital importance of passing the San Andrés Accords as a step towards peace and, more significantly, a step toward restoring dignity to

Mexico's indigenous peoples (81–2). Following the congressional address, the Zapatistas returned to Chiapas, leaving the Congress to consider the San Andrés Accords.

The massive mobilizations that accompanied the Zapatista caravan seemed to suggest that nothing short of unequivocal ratification of the original Accords would suffice; however, on 28 April the Mexican Congress passed a severely watered-down version of the negotiated agreements, ignoring key points relating to indigenous autonomy. While the Accords had been drafted by the Commission on Concordance and Pacification (COCOPA) and signed by both the government and the EZLN, the Congress rewrote the Accords substantially. The provisions for autonomy were eliminated, with 'autonomy' now being 'defined and implemented not by the indigenous peoples themselves' — a fundamental contravention of the very meaning of 'autonomy' — 'but by 31 state congresses, the most corrupt legislative level on the republic's political map' (89). Indigenous communities were also reaffirmed as socio-political entities subordinate to state governments. While the original Accords sought to devolve political power to the communities as 'entities of public right' the rewritten law referred to these same communities as 'entities of public interest', with no significant transfer of jurisdictional authority from the state to them. The principle of collective ownership of land and resources, such a central point of struggle for the Zapatistas and for Mexican campesino struggles historically, was 'erased in favor of preserving private ownership', thus facilitating the continued exploitation of indigenous territories by transnational capital (89). The capacity for indigenous communities to make decisions about social and political organization based on their own traditions was also subordinated to state and federal laws. Indigenous peoples throughout Mexico denounced the passage of this 'reform' and a broad cross-section of Mexican and international civil society protested vigorously against this betrayal of the peace process. For the Zapatistas, the actions of the Congress and Fox's administration meant that there remained no basis for continuing dialogue, and they severed all contact with the Mexican government for the duration of Fox's regime.

Following the March of the Colour of Earth and the failure of Congress to ratify the San Andrés Accords as they had been negotiated, the Zapatistas seemed to withdraw from the national and international headlines. In fact, what the Zapatistas were engaged in was the work of building relations of effective autonomy in Zapatista rebel territory in spite of the government's failure to acknowledge its existence. In this spirit, in the summer of 2003, the EZLN announced the 'death' of the five Aguascalientes — spaces of encounter between the Zapatistas and national and international civil society (Subcomandante Marcos 2004a: 593–601; see also Muñoz Ramírez 2008: 264–5). With them, declared Marcos, would die the paternalism and charity response of some members of national and international civil society that had stifled some communities' autonomy in a sea of imposed projects and leftover goods masquerading as aid (Subcomandante Marcos 2004a: 600). In their place, the Zapatistas announced the 'birth' of the 'Caracoles' — 'snail shells' — in Oventik, Morelia, Roberto Barrios, La Garrucha and La Realidad, the same communities that had housed the Aguascalientes (601–6). The Caracoles would serve as political and cultural centres, gateways into and out of Zapatista territory in rebellion, and places of encounter between the Zapatistas and national and international civil society (Muñoz Ramírez 2008: 264). Each Caracol would also bear a unique name that would identify it to the wider world. As Subcomandante Marcos explains:

The Caracol of La Realidad, of Tojolabal, Tzeltal and Mame Zapatistas, will be called 'Madre de los Caracoles del Mar de Nuestros Sueños' (Mother of Caracoles of the Sea of Our Dreams), or 'SNAN XOCH BAJ PAMAN JA TEZ WAYCHIMEL KUUNTIC'.

The Caracol of Morelia, of Tzeltal, Tzotzil and Tojolabal Zapatistas, will be called 'Torbellino de Nuestras Palabras' (Whirlwind of Our Words), or 'MUCUL PUY ZUTUIK JUN JCOPTIC'.

The Caracol of La Garrucha, of Tzeltal Zapatistas, will be called 'Resistencia Hacia un Nuevo Amancer' (Resistance for a New Dawn), or 'TE PUY TAS MALIYEL YAS PAS YACHIL SACAL QUINAL'.

The Caracol of Roberto Barrios, of Chol, Zoque and Tzeltal Zapatistas, will be called 'El Caracol Que Habla Para Todos' (The Caracol Which Speaks for All), or 'TE PUY YAX SCOPJ YUUN PISILTIC' (in Tzeltal), and 'PUY MUITITAN CHA AN TI LAK PEJTEL' (in Chol).

The Caracol of Oventik, of Tzotziles and Tzeltales, will be called 'Resistencia y Rebeldia Por la Humanidad' (Resistance and Rebellion for Humanity), or 'TA TZIKEL VOCOLIL XCHIUC JTOYBAILTIC SVENTA SLEKILAL SJUNUL BALUMIL'. (2004a: 605–6)

In addition to the birth of the Caracoles, the Zapatistas also announced the formation of the Juntas de Buen Gobierno (JBG), the Councils of Good Government, marking the fulfilment of community autonomy in Zapatista territory in rebellion. The Zapatista Autonomous Rebel Municipal Zone (MAREZ) would be administered from the Caracoles by the Juntas, with each of the Juntas including one or more representatives from each of the autonomous municipalities grouped together in each MAREZ (Ross 2006: 193). All told, the Juntas de Buen Gobierno would serve as the administrative organs overseeing five MAREZs, grouping together 29 autonomous municipalities made up of 2,222 villages and approximately 100,000 Zapatistas (194). One of the core functions of the JBGs was to mediate conflict between different autonomous municipalities within their respective jurisdictions, relieving the Clandestine Indigenous Revolutionary Committee of these responsibilities. The JBGs would even be open to non-Zapatistas living in rebel territory, thus providing a new model of governance for all peoples living in the region. A second core function of the JBGs was to ensure an equitable distribution of resources among the MAREZs and the communities that constituted them. Effectively, the Zapatistas had put into practice what the San Andrés Accords had promised but been prevented from implementing. Rather than waiting for autonomy to be bestowed upon them, the Zapatistas decided to live it.

In July 2005, after declaring a General Red Alert in Chiapas and a period of internal deliberation, the General Command of the EZLN issued a series of communiqués culminating in the 'Sixth Declaration of the Lacandón Jungle'. This newest declaration outlines an ambitious political project for the next stage in the Zapatistas' struggle, both nationally and globally. Maintaining its commitment to non-violent political action and reaffirming its subordination to the will of the indigenous communities making up its base of support, as well as its commitment to support and defend these communities, the General Command of the EZLN articulates a distinct set of plans at the global and national levels.

At the national level, the General Command outlines four goals for the next stage of struggle. First, the General Command states that the EZLN will 'continue fighting for the Indian peoples of Mexico, but now not just for them and not with only them, but for all the exploited and dispossessed of Mexico, with all of them and all over the country. And when we say all the exploited of Mexico, we are also talking about the brothers and sisters who have had to go to the United States in search of work in order to survive' (EZLN 2005). Second, the General Command affirms that they 'are going to go to listen to, and talk directly with, without intermediaries or mediation, the simple and humble of the Mexican people, and, according to what we hear and learn, we are going to go about building, along with those people who, like us, are humble and simple, a national program of struggle, but a program which will be clearly of the left, or anti-capitalist, or anti-neoliberal, or for justice, democracy and liberty for the Mexican people' (EZLN 2005). Third, the General Command asserts that

> We are going to try to build, or rebuild, another way of doing politics, one which once again has the spirit of serving others, without material interests, with sacrifice, with dedication, with honesty, which keeps its word, whose only payment is the satisfaction of duty performed, or like the militants of the left did before, when they were not stopped by blows, jail or death, let alone by dollar bills.

Fourth and finally, the General Command of the EZLN states that they are

> going to go about raising a struggle in order to demand that we make a new Constitution, new laws which take into account the demands of the Mexican people, which are: housing, land, work, food, health, education, information, culture, independence, democracy, justice, liberty and peace. A new Constitution which recognizes the rights and liberties of the people, and which defends the weak in the face of the powerful. (EZLN 2005)

Globally, the EZLN outlines three general goals: first, 'We will forge new relationships of mutual respect and support with persons and organizations who are resisting and struggling against neoliberalism and for humanity'; second, 'As far as we are able, we will send material aid such as food and handicrafts for those brothers and sisters who are struggling all over the world' — in this regard, the General Command identifies Cuba, Bolivia and Ecuador as specific destinations for material aid; third, the General Command states 'to all of those who are resisting throughout the world, we say there must be other intercontinental encuentros held, even if just one other' (EZLN 2005). These goals are articulated in the spirit of the Zapatistas' 'simple word sent out to the noble hearts of those simple and humble people who resist and rebel against injustices all over the world' (EZLN 2005).

The General Command describes the project articulated in the sixth declaration as one which seeks to build a non-electoral, broad-based alternative to 'neoliberal destruction', an alternative that is 'from below and for below' (EZLN 2005). The construction of a new kind of politics that is non-violent, non-electoral, broad-based, anti-neoliberal and anti-capitalist, and yet is nevertheless explicitly directed towards the defence of national sovereignty and concerned with the articulation of a new constitution character-izes the national — and dominant — dimension of the 'Sixth Declaration of the Lacandón Jungle'. Concluding the declaration, the General Command reaffirms both the global and the national dimensions of this new stage of the Zapatista struggle:

> In the world, we are going to join together more with the resistance struggles against neoliberalism and for humanity.
> And we are going to support, even if it's but little, those struggles.
> And we are going to exchange, with mutual respect, experiences, histories, ideas, dreams.
> In Mexico, we are going to travel all over the country, through the ruins left by the neoliberal wars and through those resistances which, entrenched, are flourishing in those ruins.
> We are going to seek, and to find, those who love these lands and these skies even as much as we do.
> We are going to seek, from La Realidad to Tijuana, those who want to organize, struggle and build what may perhaps be the last hope this Nation — which has been going on at least since the time when an eagle alighted on a nopal in order to devour a snake — has of not dying.

We are going for democracy, liberty and justice for those of us who have been denied it.

We are going with another politics, for a program of the left and for a new Constitution. (EZLN 2005)

In order to concretize the political project described in the 'Sixth Declaration of the Lacandón Jungle', the Zapatistas initiated the 'Other Campaign'. The Other Campaign, which ran parallel to the Mexican presidential campaign in 2006, sought explicitly to build a new kind of political movement of the left, from the grassroots, and outside the formal political system (see Bellinghausen and Muñoz Ramírez 2008: 317–34; Hernández Navarro 2006: 7–59). Adopting the name 'Delegate Zero', Subcomandante Marcos kicked off the campaign dramatically on the first day of 2006, the twelfth anniversary of the Zapatista uprising when, 'encased in a shiny black-visored crash helmet, mounted on a silver and black Yamaha à la Che Guevara', he raced out of the Caracol at La Garrucha (Ross 2006: 325). The first stage of the Other Campaign consisted of delegations of Zapatistas touring places throughout the Mexican nation 'to meet with leftist political organizations, landless peasants, the families of murdered women, repressed teachers, forsaken fishermen, exploited sex workers, jobless or underpaid workers, youths at risk, ostracized gays, lesbians and transgendered persons' (Bellinghausen and Muñoz Ramírez 2008: 317–18). Subcomandante Marcos — Delegate Zero — was the Zapatista to take up the first tour. The aim of this tour was to build a greater understanding of what an 'other politics' that built bridges between diverse groups in struggle might look like on the ground for the Zapatistas and for disparate pockets of dissent, dissatisfaction and potential rebellion. Marcos's tour, however, and the Other Campaign in general, did not manage to live up to the promise invested in it — at least it has yet to do so.

Touring the nation and meeting with diverse groups of people in struggle, the Other Campaign and its Delegate Zero nevertheless struggled to measure up to the drama of the Mexican presidential election. The election was hotly contested between the populist left candidate for the PRD, Andrés Manuel López Obrador, and PAN candidate Felipe Calderón, with Calderón declared the winner by the slimmest of margins, a victory tainted by allegations of fraud (Ross 2006: 368). Indeed, the campaign had been one political drama after another as the PAN and its corporate media allies sought to subvert López Obrador's candidacy at every turn. López Obrador was a former mayor of Mexico City and a moderately progressive populist who had won public admiration for his combativeness, social-democratic commitments, and unassuming lifestyle (278). Fearing another left populist leader in Latin America, López Obrador's rivals sought through legal means to invalidate his candidacy and, when that proved unsuccessful, simply to tarnish it through allegations of corruption, throughout the lead-up to the elections. The dramatic spectacle of presidential politics overshadowed Delegate Zero and the Other Campaign, both of which drew considerably smaller crowds than the Zapatistas had managed to galvanize in years past. While the Other Campaign sought to build another way of doing politics, the electoral drama proved too powerful a draw, and perhaps Marcos's solo tour too quixotic, for Mexicans to be radicalized broadly by it, and, as of this writing, no mass movement has emerged out of it. Of course, this does not mean that the Other Campaign is dead or that it will never succeed in generating a mass movement based on an 'other' politics.

Indeed, in the final days of 2008, the EZLN convoked the Global Festival of Dignified Rage in Mexico City under the banner of the Other Campaign. The Festival provided a forum for participants from Mexico and from around the world to discuss radical politics, social movements, history and analysis, under the theme of 'Another World, Another Path: Below and to the Left'. There were three stages to the Festival. The first stage took place in Mexico City on 26–29 December 2008 where 270 speakers from 57 collectives in 25 countries gave presentations while another 1,155 people from 228 organizations from 27 Mexican states presented their political and cultural proposals. Approximately 2,500 people attended the event while a hundred artistic groups 'shared their music, theater, dance, stories, poems, paintings, films, videos and photography related to the struggles in Mexico and the world' (Alonso 2009). In the mornings, attendees discussed the 'four wheels of capitalism' — exploitation, dispossession, repression and disdain — turning their attention in the afternoons to a discussion of 'other paths': 'another city, other social movements, another history and another form of politics' (Alonso 2009). The first stage of the Festival concluded with a statement condemning the Israeli Defense Force's invasion of the Gaza Strip and its subsequent massacre of Palestinians in its attempt to dismantle Hamas.

For the Festival's second stage, the event was relocated to the Oventik Caracol in Chiapas to celebrate the fifteenth anniversary of the Zapatista uprising. The Zapatistas' message was a simple one: the struggle for dignity and autonomy would continue in Chiapas and around the world even as the powerful sought to destroy those who resisted neoliberalism. The Zapatistas affirmed their continued resistance and their commitment to building a new world marked by justice, democracy and peace while calling 'on all good and honest people to join their resistances, struggles and dignified rage together in the hope that another world was possible' (Alonso 2009).

The third and final stage of the Festival took place on 2–5 January 2009, in the University of the Land in San Cristóbal de las Casas. It was organized into nine roundtables that discussed the issues of 'the other world' and 'another form of politics' and approximately 3,500 people attended. Subcomandante Marcos was in attendance at the event, as were other Zapatista leaders, including: Insurgent Lieutenant Colonel Moisés; Comandantes Tacho, Guillermo, Zebedeo and David; Comandantas Susana, Miriam, Hortensia and Florencia; Insurgent Captain Elena; and compañera Everilda (Alonso 2009). As the Global Festival of Dignified Rage demonstrates, while there remains much work to be done if the Zapatistas are to galvanize a broad-based movement in Mexico 'from below and to the left', the Other Campaign and the 'Sixth Declaration of the Lacandón Jungle' testify to the fact that the rebel spirit animating Zapatismo persists and continues to seek paths beyond the status quo.

An other Mexico

The Zapatista struggle has undergone considerable transformation since the EZLN began its rebellion in 1994. Indeed, the remarkable effects the Zapatistas have had in Mexico are due, at least in part, to the Zapatistas' own capacity to listen, to be self-critical, and to innovate as the contours of struggle change. Catalysing a diverse movement for radical socio-political change in Mexico, the Zapatistas have moved from an armed insurgency to a movement whose strength is based in a grassroots democratic politics, creative engagement and dialogue. Rather than limiting their demands to issues concerning indigenous autonomy in Chiapas, the Zapatistas have also continually insisted on the national dimensions of their struggle and have sought to engage others in Mexico accordingly. While doing so, the base communities of the EZLN have successfully consolidated relations of autonomy in Chiapas, effectively building a new social and political world in the shell of the old. The significance of the rebel spirit and example of the Zapatistas in Mexico cannot be measured simply in terms of the Zapatistas' concrete victories or their control of physical or political space. Instead, the national significance of Zapatismo can only be understood by looking at the radically reshaped Mexican political landscape — and the expanded political horizons of other radical actors in Mexico — since the Zapatistas initiated their war against oblivion.

4

'A world made of many worlds'

THE TRANSNATIONAL IMPACT
OF ZAPATISMO

ONE OF the most important features marking the Zapatistas as rebels — with all the righteousness and legitimacy that implies — instead of terrorists or other destabilizing forces is the powerful impact they have had transnationally. Far away from the concrete terrain of struggle and alternative-building occupied by the EZLN and the Zapatista movement in Mexico, Zapatismo and the Zapatista struggle have galvanized a new wave of activism and renewed hope for socio-political alternatives. As rebels on a transnational stage of political action the Zapatistas have produced diverse, multiple and often unexpected effects. How, why and with what consequences the Zapatistas have managed to achieve this kind of global significance is what I focus upon here.

From the local to the transnational:
Zapatismo beyond borders

As I discussed in the previous chapter, the significance of the Zapatista struggle in a national context has been explored from a variety of important perspectives (Aridjis 2002; Gilbreth and

Otero 2001; Gilly 1998; Hernández Navarro 2002; Leyva Solano 1998; Monsiváis 2002). However, outside of the Mexican context, the significance of the Zapatista rebellion and the role of the Zapatistas as rebels have been much less completely considered. When Zapatismo's transnational impact is seriously considered by analysts — academic and otherwise — it is all too often reduced to a matter of form, channels and structure. Most frequently this analysis is situated in relation to globalizing processes such as economic integration, technological innovation in travel and communications, and a variety of political factors supposedly characteristic of 'globalization', such as the spread of the discourse of democracy and human rights (see Knudson 1998; Olesen 2005; Tarrow 2005). The problem with understanding Zapatismo's transnational reach in these terms is that these analyses tend to lend far too much weight to the material resources and interest supplied most often by activists and observers in the world's most overdeveloped nations, while undervaluing the actual work of movement-building on the ground in any vital struggle.

Even more problematically, in what has become by now a familiar refrain, analyses such as these suggest that 'public relations' was the main weapon of the Zapatista struggle, that Marcos is a master of media manipulation, that the Zapatistas are Internet warriors, and that the uprising of 1 January 1994 was perhaps little more than a carefully managed public-relations stunt designed to draw international attention and sympathy. Such a fascination with the tools and technique of communication not only obscures the very real conditions of organizing and struggle on the ground but also presumes that the Zapatista struggle — with the very real costs implied for those who engage in it — is akin to a media spectacle designed and deployed for those who have the time, comfort, privilege and opportunity to consume it. Absent from these analyses is any kind of explicit acknowledgement that despite Marcos's savvy use of the modern media, these technologies are rare if not entirely unknown within Zapatista base communities themselves, many of which lack running water and electricity let alone television and Internet connections. Moreover, these analyses also frequently overstate the extent to which international opinion and attention have mattered to the Zapatistas in their struggle. While it would be inaccurate to ascribe no significance at all to it, had the Zapatistas relied upon the fickle attention of an international public their movement would have been crushed long ago. While one cannot deny the role of the Internet and information networks as vital tools for communication and the dissemination of information, communicative tools should not be mistaken for social action.

As anthropologist Arjun Appadurai has argued with respect to electronic media in a globalizing world, 'Part of what the mass media make *possible*, because of the conditions of collective reading, criticism, and pleasure', is the formation of a 'community of sentiment', a 'group that begins to imagine and feel things together' (1996: 8; emphasis added). While innovations in form, channel and structure provide the possibility for the diffusion of political struggle on a near global scale, it is not a substitute for it. As Eric Selbin argues, 'along with the material or structural conditions which commonly guide our investigations [into radical and revolutionary social movements], it is imperative to recognize the role played by stories, narratives of popular resistance, rebellion and revolution which have animated and emboldened generations of revolutionaries across time and cultures' (2003: 84). Understanding the influence of Zapatismo transnationally requires attending carefully to the story of a common, radical, and hopeful struggle the Zapatistas have told since 1994.

Of course, not all analyses of the role of media in relation to the transnationalization of the Zapatista struggle are reductive (see,

for example, Cleaver 1998; Russell 2005). At their most persua-
sive, these analyses focus upon the way narratives of struggle and
possibility have been effectively and widely circulated through
the use of modern communications technologies and the channels
to which they are linked. In this regard, however, issues of form,
channel and structure are clearly secondary when compared to
the significance of compelling stories of radical social change
— stories that tell us things could be otherwise. Highlighting the
powerful role electronic communications networks have played
in the linking of disparate activist groups both in support of the
Zapatista movement and in a project of resistance and alternative-
building to neoliberal capitalist globalization, the strength of
these analyses is that they do not reduce issues of mobilization,
political innovation and radical political action to issues of form,
channel or structure.

So what of my own perspective and analysis? Elsewhere, I
have examined Zapatismo as a transnational political imagination, tracing the effects of its resonance among diverse groups
of activists in the Global North (see Khasnabish 2008a, 2008b,
2007), but here I focus specifically upon the Zapatistas as rebels
on a globalized terrain of socio-political struggle. In this regard,
the rebel struggle of the Zapatistas has had special significance for
the alter-globalization movement — that 'movement of movements'
that emerged in the aftermath of the Zapatista rebellion to contest
neoliberal capitalist globalization.

In the Global North, this 'movement of movements' emerged
most spectacularly in the protests against the WTO in Seattle in
November 1999 and for many it marked the beginning of a new
cycle of radical activism. The emergence of this broad-based,
diverse and increasingly direct-action-oriented movement was
particularly significant given that it appeared in the wake of
the dissolution of the Soviet Union and the declaration of what

neoliberal ideologues at the beginning of the 1990s called 'the end of history' — the end of the clash between competing ideologies and the global ascendance of neoliberal capitalism and its trappings of an elite-driven liberal democracy. For many activists, the beginning of the final decade of the twentieth century seemed to be a very dark time as socio-political and economic alternatives to capitalism appeared almost non-existent with the collapse of state-sponsored socialism and the advance of neoliberal trade agreements in places like North America which enshrined the rights of capital over those of people and the environment. As neoconservative politicians like Ronald Reagan in the USA, Margaret Thatcher in the UK and Brian Mulroney in Canada intoned 'there is no alternative' to neoliberal capitalist globalization, and neoliberal economists and ideologues sought to provide ideological support for the statement that the world had arrived at the end of history, the Zapatistas were preparing for their war against oblivion.

When the EZLN rose up in arms on 1 January 1994 and declared the North American Free Trade Agreement to be a 'death sentence' to the indigenous peoples of Mexico, it was a shot heard around the world. In this moment of capitalist triumphalism, the Zapatista rebellion — by its very existence — testified to the enduring power of dignity and the possibility of political, economic and social alternatives to the dominant order. With no pre-existing ties to activist groups beyond the borders of Mexico, in the days following the uprising the Zapatista struggle would begin to infiltrate the political imaginations of diverse groups of people around the world. Indeed, beyond providing a concrete, tactical example of dedicated resistance to a supposedly inevitable project of capitalist development, the Zapatista rebellion provided people around the world with a powerful example of hope and dignity in the darkest of times.

In the aftermath of the uprising, the EZLN would remain limited to rebel territory in the state of Chiapas — hemmed in by tens of thousands of Mexican military troops — and the Zapatista movement would remain focused within Mexican national territory. In spite of this, Zapatismo would travel via activist solidarity delegations, conventional corporate news sources, academic analyses, and a variety of other — and particularly digital — media far beyond these borders. While the Zapatistas explicitly sought to galvanize Mexican society into a broad-based rebellion against the existing corrupt power structure in the country, nothing in the EZLN's initial statements or declarations indicated their rebellion was in any way aimed at attracting the attention of an international audience. Nevertheless, people the world over would respond passionately to the Zapatista rebellion. At first, the response mirrored the initial Mexican national response, with diverse groups organizing aid and solidarity caravans to Chiapas in addition to protesting outside of Mexican embassies against the Mexican government's treatment of the Zapatistas. In the weeks, months and years that would follow, however, the transnational engagement with Zapatismo would become more diverse, much less traditionally solidaristic in nature, and much more attuned to building what the Zapatistas would call an 'international order of hope for humanity and against neoliberalism' in the midst of the Fourth World War.

Rebels and the Fourth World War

The Zapatistas have long asserted that the time and space we are now living through are those of 'the Fourth World War'. While the Third World War, otherwise known as the Cold War, ended with the collapse of the Soviet Union and the 'victory' of neoliberal capitalism over state-sponsored socialism, the Fourth World War marks a time when global neoliberal capitalism has ushered in 'a new framework of international relations in which the new struggle for … new markets and territories' has produced 'a new world war', a war against humanity (Subcomandante Marcos 2004d: 257). Rather than national armies facing off against one another or, to invoke a more recent elite imaginary, a geographically and temporally unlimited police action against shadowy terrorist cells, this world war is one of a geopolitical system and its agents, armies and weapons — military, socio-political and economic — versus the vast majority of humanity. While many have yet actively to enter this war — choosing instead to see systems of political, social and economic domination under which they live either as natural or as unavoidable — there are others the world over who not only continue to be marginalized and targeted by this system but are actively seeking to resist and build alternatives to it. As Marcos writes:

> That is what this is all about. It is war. A war against humanity. The globalization of those who are above us is nothing more than a global machine that feeds on blood and defecates in dollars.
>
> In the complex equation that turns death into money, there is a group of humans who command a very low price in the global slaughterhouse. We are the indigenous, the young, the women, the children, the elderly, the homosexuals, the migrants, all those who are different.
>
> That is to say, the immense majority of humanity.
>
> This is a world war of the powerful who want to turn the planet into a private club that reserves the right to refuse admission. The exclusive luxury zone where they meet is a microcosm of their project for the planet, a complex of hotels, restaurants, and recreation zones protected by armies and police forces.
>
> All of us are given the option of being inside this zone, but only as servants. Or we can remain outside of the world, outside of life. But we have no reason to obey and accept this choice between living as servants or dying. We can build a new path, one where living

means life with dignity and freedom. To build this alternative is possible and necessary. It is necessary because on it depends the future of humanity.

This future is up for grabs in every corner of each of the five continents. This alternative is possible because around the world people know that liberty is a word which is often used as an excuse for cynicism.

Brothers and sisters, there is dissent over the projects of globalization all over the world. Those above, who globalize conformism, cynicism, stupidity, war, destruction and death. And those below who globalize rebellion, hope, creativity, intelligence, imagination, life, memory, and the construction of a world that we can all fit in, a world with democracy, liberty and justice. (2004c: 626–7)

This is not a struggle engaged in by a homogeneous group of people, it is not a struggle built according to strict principles or a revolutionary blueprint; it is rather a struggle that is being joined by rebels all over the world seeking to affirm their autonomy and interconnectedness, their will to live in a world capable of holding many worlds.

Absent from the quotation above and from other Zapatista efforts at constructing and communicating this new politics of radical possibility are the more familiar tropes of socialist ideology and rhetoric such as the proletariat, the masses, the vanguard, the revolutionary state, and the progressive path from capitalism to socialism to communism. In the midst of this world war, in place of the familiar modern revolutionary actors and narratives, we find something very different:

The apparent infallibility of globalization comes up hard against the stubborn disobedience of reality. While neoliberalism is pursuing its war, groups of protesters, kernels of rebels, are forming throughout the planet. The empire of financiers with full pockets confronts the rebellion of pockets of resistance. Yes, pockets. Of all sizes, of different colors, of varying shapes. Their sole common point is a desire to resist the 'New World Order' and the crime against humanity that is represented by this Fourth World War. (Subcomandante Marcos 2002b: 282)

In this communiqué Marcos poetically describes the emergence of what would become known as the alter-globalization 'movement of movements' as one made up of 'kernels of rebels' and a 'rebellion of pockets of resistance'. In this way, the Zapatistas conceptualize their own rebellion as connected to that of others in different parts of the world. Instead of casting their path of struggle as the true one leading to liberation, the Zapatistas evoke a notion of resistance and alternative-building that is fundamentally expansive and unpredictable — one that in every place will necessarily look different as it responds to the needs and desires of the people bringing it into being. Nevertheless, these pockets of rebellion are conceived of as fundamentally interconnected as they confront a global system of neoliberal capitalism that seeks to map, exploit and dominate them.

Marcos's eloquent rhetoric aside, how can the significance of Zapatismo transnationally be traced? How, ultimately, can one 'see' the impact of this rebel struggle and its attendant political philosophy and practice on people engaged in their own struggles far beyond the borders of Chiapas? One way to appreciate this is by attending to the words of activists themselves and listening attentively to the ways in which they narrate the importance of Zapatismo in relation to their own struggles and their understanding of the alter-globalization movement. Turning to some of the writing that has emerged from the ranks of the alter-globalization movement provides a written archive of the transnational significance of Zapatismo for rebels everywhere.

So if we turn to this archive, what do we find? In the words of Paul Kingsnorth, 'The Zapatistas would become the unwitting, but not unwilling, forgers of a truly global insurgency against history's first truly global system' (2003: 7). Or, as scholar and activist Manuel Callahan contends, 'In many respects the Zapatista uprising is the moment when the movement against globalization found its global audience, and it is perhaps the place where the tactics of that movement began' (2004a: 12). The importance of Zapatismo to the alter-globalization movement is perhaps most powerfully captured by the editorial collective Notes From Nowhere in *We Are Everywhere: The Irresistible Rise of Global Anticapitalism* (2003). In the first entry of their timeline of global anti-capitalism entitled 'The Restless Margins: Moments of Resistance and Rebellion' the editorial collective writes of 1 January 1994, 'The EZLN ... declares war against Mexico, bringing its inspirational struggle for life and humanity to the forefront of political imaginations across the planet' (2003: 31). Elaborating upon this inspiration, Notes From Nowhere proceed to explain the relationship between the rebel ethic of Zapatismo and the global anti-capitalist movement, as well as to situate it historically:

> Movements of the past are laden with charismatic leaders — Che Guevara, Rosa Luxemburg, Huey Newton, Karl Marx, Emma Goldman, Lenin, Mao Tse-Tung. But whose face can be found in the foreground of today's movement? Ironically, the first face that comes to mind is masked and bears the pseudonym 'Subcomandante Marcos'. This is the spokesperson for the Zapatistas, whose words have profoundly influenced the spirit of the movement. But he, like so much of this movement, thrives on the power and creativity of paradox, for he speaks of leading by obeying, carrying out the policies of a committee of indigenous campesinos. Note the 'sub'commander, and the anonymity of the mask. He warns that the name Marcos is interchangeable — anyone can put on a ski mask and say 'I am Marcos'. In fact he says that Marcos does not exist, but is simply a window, a bridge, a mediator between worlds. He says that we are all Marcos. Not what one expects from a traditional leader.
>
> It follows that a movement with no leaders organizes horizontally, through networks. And it was the poetic communiqués and powerful

stories that trickled from the Zapatista autonomous zones in the Chiapas jungle onto the relatively new medium of the internet which told of their suffering, their struggles, their mythologies, that began to weave an electronic fabric of struggle in the mid-nineties. This web of connections between diverse groups gave birth to a series of face-to-face international gatherings — the Zapatista Encuentros — which soon grew to become the roaring, unstoppable torrent of movements for life and dignity and against capital that are emerging across the world. 'We are the network,' declared the Zapatistas, 'all of us who resist.' (64–5)

Journalist and activist Naomi Klein has considered what she labels 'the Zapatista effect', asking 'what are the ideas that proved so powerful that thousands have taken it on themselves to disseminate them around the world?' (2002: 219). She answers: 'They have to do with power — and new ways of imagining it' (219). While Klein discusses the importance of the Zapatistas' emphasis upon democracy, liberty and justice in addition to their disavowal of the desire to seize state power as fundamental aspects of Zapatismo's global appeal, she also speaks to its fundamentally rebellious character: 'This is the essence of Zapatismo, and explains much of its appeal: a global call to revolution that tells you not to wait for the revolution, only to start where you stand, to fight with your own weapon' (220–21). Perhaps even more significantly, Klein ends by reflecting on Marcos and the Zapatistas as rebels in relation to a wider history of political struggle in order to situate their appeal and relevance:

> As I listened to Marcos address the crowds in Mexico City [during the Zapatistas' March of Indigenous Dignity in 2001], I was struck that he didn't sound like a politician at a rally or a preacher at a pulpit, he sounded like a poet — at the world's largest poetry reading. And it occurred to me then that Marcos actually isn't Martin Luther King Jr.; he is King's very modern progeny, born of a bittersweet marriage of vision and necessity. This masked man who calls

himself Marcos is the descendant of King, Che Guevara, Malcolm X, Emiliano Zapata and all the other heroes who preached from pulpits only to be shot down one by one, leaving bodies of followers wandering around blind and disoriented because they had lost their heads. And in their place, the world has a new kind of hero, one who listens more than he speaks, who preaches in riddles not in certainties, a leader who doesn't show his face, who says his mask is really a mirror. And in the Zapatistas we have not one dream of a revolution but a dreaming revolution. 'This is our dream,' writes Marcos, 'the Zapatista paradox — one that takes away sleep. The only dream that is dreamed awake, sleepless. The history that is born and nurtured from below.' (223)

While the archive of writings emerging from the alter-globalization movement offers many more reflections on the significance of the Zapatista rebellion, I will limit my survey of them to one more perspective. Rebecca Solnit, author and US-based activist, offers a compelling perspective on Zapatismo and its global significance that also bears quoting at length:

In dazzling proclamations and manifestos, the Zapatistas announced the rise of the fourth world and their radical rejection of neoliberalism. They were never much of a military force, but their intellectual and imaginative power has been staggering ... [The Zapatistas] came not just to enact a specific revolution but to bring a revolution, so to speak, in the nature of revolutions. They critiqued the dynamics of power, previous revolutions, capitalism, colonialism, militarism, sexism, racism, and occasionally Marxism, recognizing the interplay of many forces and agendas in any act, any movement. They were nothing so simple as socialists, and they did not posit the old vision of state socialism as a solution to the problems of neoliberalism. They affirmed women's full and equal rights, refusing to be the revolution that sacrifices or postpones one kind of justice for another. They did not attempt to export their revolution but invited others to find their own local version of it, and from their forests and villages they entered into conversation with the world through encuentros, or encounters — conferences of a sort — communiqués,

emissaries, and correspondence. For the rest of us, the Zapatistas
came as a surprise and as a demonstration that overnight, the most
marginal, overlooked place can become the center of the world.

They were not just demanding change, but embodying it; and in
this, they were and are already victorious ... They understood the
interplay between physical actions, those carried out with guns, and
symbolic actions, those carried out with rods, with images, with art,
with communications, and they won through the latter means what
they never could have won through their small capacity for violence.
(2004: 34–5)

I have surveyed this written archive of Zapatismo's significance from the perspective of northern activists engaged in the
alter-globalization movement not to suggest that they are perfect
descriptions of the essence of Zapatismo but rather to offer them
as particularly eloquent reflections on Zapatismo as a rebel struggle of global significance. Far from being seen merely as insurgents, these passages situate the Zapatistas and Zapatismo as vital
pieces of a global rebellion against neoliberal capitalism and elite
domination of people and the planet. Of course, these perspectives on the Zapatistas as rebels of transnational significance also
foreground elements of the Zapatista struggle while downplaying
others. Prominent in these articulate passages are notions of hope,
inclusivity, imagination, dignity, communication, democracy, and
a radical sense of possibility. As I detailed in Chapter 2, these
elements are most certainly present in Zapatismo — and even
more so with respect to the communiqués and communicative
actions directed towards supporters transnationally — but their
prominence in these passages also speak to the context and position from which each of these writers comes.

The emphasis upon a powerful rejection of neoliberalism, the
affirmation of human dignity, peace, autonomy and interconnectedness, and the desire for dialogue, coupled with a valorization of
communicative and symbolic action rather than violent insurrec-

tion cannot be divorced from the predominantly Northern context from which these activists write. This has always been a problematic dynamic as people view movements elsewhere through the lens of their own desire for change and their own understandings of struggle, and this has certainly happened with respect to the Zapatistas (see Hellman 2000; Meyer 2002). However, this ambiguity has also been a fundamental element of the Zapatistas' rebel appeal. In transmitting Zapatismo to people living, working and struggling outside of the indigenous communities of Chiapas, Marcos's writing in particular has foregrounded those elements of Zapatista discourse most likely to speak compellingly across a variety of disparate contexts. In addition, activists outside of Chiapas have also actively participated in reading the Zapatista struggle from their own position, a reading necessarily coloured by one's own experience. None of this makes the encounter between activists transnationally and the Zapatistas — however this encounter has been mediated — inauthentic. Rather, it suggests that the significance of the Zapatistas as rebels on a transnational political scale has to be understood less in terms of a monologue-like 'inspiration' and more as a dynamic dialogue given shape by the contexts within which it occurs.

An international order of hope: transnational encounters with Zapatismo

The encounters between other pockets of rebels on a transnational scale with Zapatismo and the Zapatista struggle have yielded a multitude of political projects since 1994 (see Khasnabish 2008b). From human rights observation groups who travel to Chiapas in order to document the abuses levelled against Zapatista communities to radical film-making collectives who take their inspiration from Zapatismo in order to tell new and inspiring stories of struggle and possibility to direct-action groups contesting neo-liberalism learning from the Zapatista example of resistance, the outcomes of these encounters have been incredibly diverse. While some groups have arisen around the world to coordinate political and material solidarity with the Zapatistas in Chiapas, others have taken the provocation of Zapatismo and sought to create their own pocket of resistance against the Fourth World War while linking their struggle explicitly to the Zapatistas. Examples of both these types are too numerous to list, but in what follows I engage two particularly compelling examples of the possibilities animated by the transnational resonance of Zapatismo: Peoples' Global Action (PGA) and Big Noise Tactical (BNT). Indeed, PGA and BNT are powerful examples of the Zapatistas as rebels on a transnational scale engaged in galvanizing other rebel pockets of resistance. To demonstrate the powerful effect Zapatismo has had transnationally, in this section I turn to the insights shared with me in interviews with PGA and BNT activists with whom I have worked over the past decade.

PEOPLES' GLOBAL ACTION

From 27 July to 3 August 1996, nearly 5,000 people from forty-two countries participated in the First Intercontinental Encuentro for Humanity and Against Neoliberalism held in Zapatista territory in rebellion (Notes From Nowhere 2003: 34; Muñoz Ramírez 2008: 144). The term *encuentro* translates in English as 'encounter' but it signifies just as much about the process and nature of these encounters as it refers to the act of meeting others. Convoked by the Zapatistas and held in the five Zapatista 'Aguascalientes' — spaces for encounter between the Zapatistas and national and international civil societies — in the communities of Oventik, La Realidad, La Garrucha, Morelia and Roberto Barrios, the first Encuentro was an opportunity for others from around the world to express directly their solidarity with the EZLN and the Zapatistas. More importantly, the Encuentro was envisioned as an explicit attempt to build a transnational network of resistances to neoliberal capitalism. As pre-eminent symbols of this kind of resistance, the Zapatistas took the opportunity to catalyse a broader movement 'for humanity and against neoliberalism' without seeking to lead it. As Paul Kingsnorth relates, 'The Encuentro sent Zapatismo global. The ... delegates returned to their countries with new ideas, new ways of thinking about the future, and above all, new links' (2003: 37). The model and inspiration of the Zapatista Encuentro in 1996 provided the spark for people from all over the world, who then went home and tried to infuse their own spaces and practices with the same joy of rebellion and hope for another world. As Fiona Jeffries, activist, writer, academic and participant in the First Intercontinental Encuentro, noted during our conversation in Vancouver, British Colombia, in the winter of 2004:

> the Encuentro was just the most amazing experience politically. That level of organization, totally outside of the state, and this amazing mobilization of people from around the world who organized this event and the people I met there [were] just so inspiring [as was] the level of debate, the level of discussion about politics. We really felt actually that some big change was going to happen, people from everywhere talking about this world as it is in so many different ways and on so many different levels and this incredible inclusion, this level of pluralism that I've never experienced before on the left. So then we came back here and we started [an] organizing process, what we were calling an 'International of Hope' because at the end [of the Encuentro] the Zapatistas said 'okay, this is what we need you to do, we need solidarity but because we're in a crisis what's real solidarity for us is to go back to where you are and organize around anti-neoliberal stuff; we're doing our thing here, you gotta do your thing here, we all gotta do our thing and hopefully that will coalesce in powerful ways.'

At the end of the first Encuentro, the General Command of the EZLN issued the 'Second Declaration of La Realidad for Humanity and Against Neoliberalism', calling for the creation of a 'collective network of all our particular struggles and resistances, an intercontinental network of resistance against neoliberalism, an intercontinental network of resistance for humanity' (EZLN 2001c: 125). Specifying that this network would not be 'an organizing structure', that it would have 'no central head or decision maker', 'no central command or hierarchies', the EZLN called for the formation of a network that would provide channels of communication and support for the diverse struggles 'for humanity and against neoliberalism' around the world (125). Peoples' Global Action (PGA) would be the network that emerged from this call — but not yet. In the 'Second Declaration of La Realidad for Humanity and Against Neoliberalism', the Zapatistas also called for a second Encuentro to be held, this time on another continent. The Second Intercontinental Encuentro for Humanity and Against Neoliberalism was held one year after the first, this time in Spain, drawing 3,000 activists from fifty countries (Flood 2003: 74). It would be at the Second Encuentro that the idea for PGA would be born out of a 'need to create something more tangible than the encuentros' (Notes From Nowhere 2003: 96). In this spirit, PGA was born at a meeting in Geneva in February 1998 with 300 activists from seventy-one countries present (Kingsnorth 2003: 73). As Olivier de Marcellus, one of the participants involved in the founding meetings of PGA, explains:

> PGA is an offshoot of the international Zapatista movement, founded in a meeting that prolonged the Second Encuentro in southern Spain, and drawing a lot of its European support from people who also support the Zapatistas. There is also a certain ideological and organizational resemblance, both being rather unorthodox, eclectic networks attempting to stimulate radical opposition worldwide. The

principal difference is that PGA aims beyond debate and exchange to propose action campaigns against neoliberalism, worldwide. (2001: 105)

Since its founding in February 1998, Peoples' Global Action has been one of the most important networks for coordination and communication among groups and individuals committed to anti-capitalist and alter-globalization action. PGA has been involved in coordinating Global Days of Action — the spectacular summit protests — against the World Trade Organization, the G8 and the World Bank, as well as a variety of conferences, caravans and workshops around the world (PGA, 'Brief History', n.d.; see also Wood 2004). It is, in essence, a rebel network inspired by the rebellious spirit and example of the Zapatista movement.

Dave Bleakney is a member of the Canadian Union of Postal Workers (CUPW) and another activist involved in the founding of Peoples' Global Action and its manifestation in North America. CUPW actually served as the regional convenor for Peoples' Global Action in North America from 1998 to 1999, a role taken over by the Montreal-based Anti-Capitalist Convergence (CLAC) after 1999. During our interview in the winter of 2004, Bleakney registered the profound value of the lessons offered by Zapatismo to Canadian and US activists since 1994. For Dave, the resonance of Zapatismo conveyed powerful lessons regarding the character and contours of struggle, as well as challenging dominant liberal notions of how politics is done and what other possibilities might look like:

> [The] struggle [of the Zapatistas] and others have taught me that we have more to learn from movements like that than they have from us. [We] need to learn from the South as opposed to [believing that] we have the answers; that's a real struggle and it gets disheartening sometimes because I think it's a real hard one to cross over. I know within the labour movement, people call it solidarity but in fact you

look at it [and] it's like charity. Labour movements [in the north] have come to maintain the order. If you look at global bodies like the WTO there's a constant clamour to get a seat at the table as if somehow being present at your own execution, surrounded by executioners, is [an] achievement. It's a really crucial juncture because — let's face it — the unions in Canada are going to be a lot more excited about going to Geneva to meet with the WTO than they are going to live off rice and beans in Chiapas for three weeks and not having any running water, but it's clear to me that the greatest lessons to be learned are from the Zapatistas, but also the *piqueteros* in Argentina who occupy factories and the MST who occupy land in Brazil. Another thing that the Zapatistas teach us is to be resourceful and self-reliant, to not think that there's somebody that's going to take care of us. I think the Zapatistas open up a whole other area of relations around the importance of honesty, that you don't need to spin anything.

The notion of the Zapatistas as teachers to political movements and activists elsewhere is a provocative one. As Bleakney points out here, ever since the fall of the Berlin Wall and the proclamation of 'the end of history' political elites have heralded liberal democracy as the pinnacle of political expression. Through their ongoing rebellion, the Zapatistas have accomplished a powerful interrogation of that conclusion, as well as a complete subversion of the dogma of 'there is no alternative'.

Very clear in its role as a network of coordination rather than an organization, PGA has served to bring diverse groups and struggles together in a spirit of explicit anti-capitalism. PGA has no membership, it represents no one, and no one is charged with representing it; it is a network comprising diverse organizations and has minimal central organizing structures, with its conferences serving as the primary collective decision-making mechanisms (PGA, 'Organisational Principles', n.d.). The overall success and sustainability of PGA is rooted in a constant decentralization of power and continual rearticulation of collective identity (Wood 2004). PGA's 'Manifesto' and 'Hallmarks' are 'living documents', subject to revision at each gathering, and facilitating the continual reinvention of collective identity, while PGA's commitment to decentralizing power and decision-making to the most immediate and immanent level (with regions responsible for deciding upon convenors and infopoints) has provided mechanisms for challenging the power hierarchies that exist in so many activist groups. PGA's 'Hallmarks' reflect its radically democratic, confrontational, and explicitly anti-capitalist spirit. As I have already noted, the 'Hallmarks', just like the 'Manifesto', are subject to revision at PGA gatherings and have in fact undergone changes at both the Bangalore and Cochabamba conferences. The 'Hallmarks' as they are currently constituted are as follows:

1. A very clear rejection of capitalism, imperialism and feudalism, and all trade agreements, institutions and governments that promote destructive globalisation.
2. We reject all forms and systems of domination and discrimination including, but not limited to, patriarchy, racism and religious fundamentalism of all creeds. We embrace the full dignity of all human beings.
3. A confrontational attitude, since we do not think that lobbying can have a major impact in such biased and undemocratic organisations, in which transnational capital is the only real policy-maker.
4. A call to direct action and civil disobedience, support for social movements' struggles, advocating forms of resistance which maximise respect for life and oppressed people's rights, as well as the construction of local alternatives to global capitalism.
5. An organisational philosophy based on decentralisation and autonomy. (PGA, 'Hallmarks', n.d.)

While PGA has faced and continues to face serious challenges in terms of serving as a transnational coordinating network of anti-capitalist action, these mechanisms have allowed it not only to survive but to coordinate an impressive list of actions. De Marcellus explains what lies at the root of this success:

> PGA has aroused amazing enthusiasm in very diverse quarters around the world, no doubt because (following the lead of the Zapatistas) it attracted many who had been waiting for such an inclusive but radical anti-capitalist appeal. Co-ordinating neither parties nor NGOs, but autonomous, grassroots movements, PGA has opened a new political space that could give an international projection and a larger political significance to the struggles of these movements. There has been a real 'circulation of struggles': the Indians inspiring the Genevans or Britons, who in turn inspire young Americans to do even better … a process of mutual discovery that started with the second Zapatista-inspired Encuentro in Spain, when Reclaim the Streets and other activists of continental Europe, for example, discovered each other. (2001: 113–14)

A network of pockets of resistance in rebellion against neoliberal capitalist globalization and its attendant structures of militarization, domination and imperialism: this is what PGA is and what the Zapatistas have served to catalyse on a transnational political stage. Without the rebel example of the Zapatistas, it is indisputable that the transnational fabric of radical struggle against neoliberal globalization would look vastly different today.

Friederike Haberman, journalist, activist, participant in both Zapatistas-inspired Encuentros, and active in Peoples' Global Action, expressed the revelatory significance of Zapatismo as well as the tangible lessons Zapatismo has offered to movements elsewhere during our interview in winter 2004. Specifically, Haberman discussed the connection between new ways of speaking and thinking about politics and the strategies used to materialize these alternatives:

a new language is important because it's easily accessible and … it's able to bridge between more theoretical discourse and a discourse everybody understands. This is another very interesting point for me because Marcos is saying this came out of a clash between the smaller group of left-wing intellectuals who came into the jungle and tried to explain to the indigenous about imperialism, and the indigenous said well what are you talking about? [Zapatismo] is what [has been] born out of [the clash of these traditions]. Subcomandante Marcos [is an interesting figure in this regard] because he speaks of 'us', of 'us indigenous', but of course he's not indigenous. It's not by [accident] that it's him who is the [Zapatistas' spokesperson] because he can reach the people of his identity, [people from the world] he has been born in, he has been educated in, but still he shifted his identity so he's not just a middle-class white guy. For me, this is a good example of how politics can become fruitful because when you're working for a better world you're always in danger to know it better for others. … [The Zapatistas make it clear that] you can't copy a [political] tactic or a [social change strategy] but what you can have are these resonances [between different struggles which can inspire you] to [take action] in a different way — and in your own way — inspired by the Zapatistas, to [act] in a self-organized way, not to expect anything from the state, not to do any lobby politics.

As expressed here, the transnationalization of Zapatismo has conveyed the notion that it is possible to build a new world today in a collective and self-organized fashion without seeking concessions from power. What it has not provided is a blueprint or guidebook to radical social transformation. In this sense, the Zapatista struggle is a catalyst for rebellion and an inspiring example of social change, not a template to be exported to other contexts.

BIG NOISE TACTICAL

PGA is a compelling and complex instance of the materialization of the impact of Zapatismo on a transnational political scale. On the transnational terrain PGA has worked to build powerful and militant manifestations of anti-capitalist struggle out of the resonance of Zapatismo and the Zapatista-inspired Encuentros. But in addition to this example of anti-capitalist networking and mobilizing, Zapatismo has also had considerable and unanticipated effects at the intersection of culture and politics outside of Mexico. Big Noise Tactical, a radical film-making collective based in New York City, is perhaps one of the most interesting examples of the unanticipated consequences of Zapatismo beyond the borders of rebel territory in Chiapas. BNT produced *Zapatista*, their first film, in 1998. This was followed by a number of other feature documentaries, including *This is What Democracy Looks Like* (2000), and *The Fourth World War* (2003), in addition to a host of 'tactical media' pieces produced in collaboration with other artists/activists focusing on a diverse set of events and issues relating to the global anti-capitalist/global justice movement. Big Noise Tactical was also a part of the first Independent Media Centre video team at the WTO protests in Seattle in 1999, providing unprecedented independent media coverage of the 'Battle of Seattle'. The activist media-makers who constitute BNT very explicitly do not situate themselves as 'documentary-makers', 'artists' or 'filmmakers'; instead, they understand their political engagement in the following way:

> We are not filmmakers producing and distributing our work. We are rebels, crystallizating radical community and weaving a network of skin and images, of dreams and bone, of solidarity and connection against the isolation, alienation and cynicism of capitalist decomposition.
>
> We are tactical because our media is a part of movements, imbedded in a history of struggle. Tactical because we are provisional, plural, polyvocal. Tactical because it would be the worst kind of arrogance to believe that our media had some ahistorical power to change the world — its only life is inside of movements — and they will hang our images on the walls of their banks if our movements do not tear their banks down. (Big Noise Tactical n.d.)

This radical commitment to producing cinematic interventions that are part of the fabric of social struggle rather than simply 'about' it clearly animates the films of Big Noise Tactical. From *Zapatista* to *The Fourth World War* — both documentaries profoundly connected to the Zapatista struggle in Chiapas and its significance beyond its own physical location — the films produced by BNT do not simply document events but participate in the formation of new subjectivities — new ways of understanding oneself and one's place in the world — and facilitate the emergence of new possibilities of connection and struggle.

The origins of Big Noise Tactical are intimately connected to Zapatismo. Rick Rowley, one of the founding members of this collective, found himself in Mexico in 1995 just as the Zapatista uprising, and the Mexican state's repression of it, were once more shaking the country. The uprising and what it represented constituted a moment of radical change for Rowley. Reflecting upon the connections between this and the formation of Big Noise Tactical, Rick explained the impact Zapatismo had upon him and the other members of the collective, during our interview in the fall of 2004:

we all accepted that invitation to become Zapatistas and we returned to the United States as Zapatistas looking for what that might mean in the north and trying to learn from their example of struggle — you know, take it seriously, not just as an inspiration but to learn from their tactics and their strategy. One of the things that was most resonant to us at that moment was the famous Zapatista line 'our word is our weapon', armed with our word and sticks against this machine we're winning, and so we thought about what our word would look like in the north and we didn't think that communiqués and children's stories and poems in the left-wing papers in the States was the move that would make sense; we thought video made sense as a language that could circulate through these circuits of American culture. None of us had ever held video cameras before [or] had any film training, but we got credit cards and we bought cameras and went down and started to shoot *Zapatista* and so that was the beginning of Big Noise, that was the beginning of the work that followed, the work that I've done since then. We've never thought of ourselves as film-makers but as Zapatistas looking for forms of struggle that make sense in the north.

Rowley and other activists with BNT have found ways not simply to 'import' Zapatismo to the USA but to find in its resonance meaning for struggles there. Through their encounter with the Zapatista struggle, BNT has engaged in the innovative process of making sense of Zapatismo's lessons and inspiration in ways that are capable of moving powerfully and dynamically through the 'circuits of American culture'.

Jacquie Soohen, another key BNT activist and film-maker, reflected upon her own encounter with Zapatismo and its consequences for herself and for her political commitments during our conversation in the fall of 2004. Building upon Rowley's comments about the search for weapons that would make sense for struggles in the North, Soohen elaborated upon the connections between politics, culture and media and their intersection with Zapatismo from the perspective of her own experience:

> [I heard] about [the Zapatista struggle] and [I was] just amazed that you could take that inspiration, the idea of victory, the idea of standing up for something and fighting and winning. You knew that the demos didn't work, you knew that it had to be something else, beyond identity politics, and taking possession of a history that was both your own and expanded beyond [the] identity boundaries that were clearly marked for you inside a world of individualistic capitalism. I went down for the second half of that shoot; [I] hadn't even thought about making films, that's not what I'd ever trained to do or even thought about doing, but when we [finished] *Zapatista* we started thinking about this and imagining this, how is our word our weapon? It was when we finally started screening the film that it began to make sense as a weapon and became something that we decided to keep doing as long as it made sense because you'd go places

and you weren't talking to people who had, for the most part, ever even heard of Zapatismo, or for the most part they weren't politically active … [but] people were so moved by it … we came to realize that it was our weapon that we could use and something we could give over to a larger movement. … It's arrogant to believe that any film or any piece of work like that is ever going to change things by itself because that's not how it functions; all of these things function inside of movements. [*Zapatista*] came out and we were working in tune with a whole bunch of people who were being inspired by the Zapatistas because it was so different and new and because it was a victory that was something that people were winning.

These compelling reflections from Rowley and Soohen illuminate some of the most interesting and unpredictable contours of the transnational significance of Zapatismo. While solidarity activism both within and outside of Mexico has been instrumental in defending the Zapatistas and their project of radical socio-political transformation, Zapatismo has also inspired activists to search for new ways of practising politics in their own spaces. Indeed, the implications of the transnational resonance of Zapatismo may quite possibly be much more powerful, and much more enduring, than the solidarity marshalled over the years by national and international 'civil societies'.

Provoked by their experience with Zapatismo to consider what weapons against neoliberalism might make sense in the north, activists involved in BNT have, much like Marcos, engaged in a struggle that is as much about ideas as it is about physical acts of resistance or alternative-building. Informational politics — and struggles over them — have been a part of political action since the first propaganda was distributed, but in a media-saturated and ever more densely interconnected society struggles over the *meaning of things* have acquired increasing importance. Jacquie Soohen reflected on this shift and the significance of Zapatismo in relation to it when she noted:

so much of the activism in the 1970s and 1980s and this whole idea of solidarity activism was ... if you just show the truth then that will ... overcome something and ... it's about speaking truth to power but ... I think we're entering a whole different time, and the Zapatistas made it clear too that it wasn't just about this media blockade, it wasn't just about the information not getting out there, it was about this ideological encirclement and how do you break that? So in the same way [our] films ... are not about speaking truth to power in that way ... especially *The Fourth World War*, it's about ... creating myths ... inside this movement and connecting connections and connectivities, like a connection-making machine ... between these different movements and also ... speaking in a way that shows our humanity and the world that we want ... things that are all beautiful and that create our own language and we start to create our own language in different ways and touch people in different ways, as opposed to taking the language ... of the powerful and using it to just show information because ... if there's anything we've learned and we learn more everyday ... it's not just ... about the information, especially now, it's about ... how it's interpreted and used and how people are made to feel connected or disconnected from it.

As Soohen makes clear here, the issue is not about getting access to 'the right' information; rather, what is at stake is the way that *meaning is made*. This is not merely an individual matter; it is a systemic and collective one. The power of Big Noise Tactical's work, as with Zapatismo transnationally, is not in its subversive content precisely but rather resides in the fact that both are directed towards the cultivation of new stories, new fabrics of communication, capable of developing new political projects, imaginations, practices and subjectivities.

Big Noise Tactical's film *The Fourth World War* is a film ostensibly about the diverse struggles that make up the 'movement of movements' that is the alter-globalization movement. Named in explicit reference to the notion of 'the Fourth World War' articulated by Subcomandante Marcos and the Zapatistas in regard to global neoliberalism (see Subcomandante Marcos 2002b), *The Fourth World War* is a film about the power of people acting collectively to change their worlds. Not a conventional documentary narrative that aims to 'tell the truth' about the alter-globalization movement, *The Fourth World War* traces the global circulation of anti-capitalist and radically democratic struggles 'for humanity and against neoliberalism'. It is also a powerful and provocative example of the materialization of a radical new way of thinking about socio-political change deeply inspired by Zapatismo. Not aiming to reproduce Zapatismo, the film takes the viewer on a whirlwind trip around the world, setting down frequently to explore an emerging global movement which is self-consciously global and yet everywhere takes on its own unique contours. While *The Fourth World War* tells a powerful story of the hope and possibility that reside in collective action for radical, anti-neoliberal social change, the film itself is an artefact of this story, it is itself a vehicle for the making of new meanings and the cultivation of new forms of struggle deeply inspired by movements like the Zapatistas. In this sense, the film is a mechanism for communication and the proliferation of radical possibilities. As Rick Rowley explained during our conversation:

Films don't change the world, movements of people do, and our films succeed or fail inasmuch ... as they participate in movements that successfully challenge this system. On one level we were ... a tissue for communication across ... geographic, political, cultural distance, we're a tissue through which it is possible for rebellious and revolutionary images to circulate, for models and tactics to circulate ... but we're part of a process that movements ... are already undertaking. It was amazing in these last couple of years to work on *The Fourth World War* and to see the degree to which movements are already in communication with one another and are self-consciously articulating themselves as global. ... We're run through by each other's ... examples and we're given strength and hope by each other's examples of victory. That's one of the things I think that movements here now, in the States especially now, need to remember … that we're a global movement and we're a historical movement, that … we're tied to people outside of our borders and to moments outside of our time … we're part of something much bigger than any state that's locked down. One of our most important roles is to remind people over and over again to fight against what I think … is the primary or most disempowering aspect of capitalist culture and the way that capitalist culture reproduces itself which is producing the feeling in each and every person that they're alone, that they're an isolated consumer who's … capable of winning victories … only alone … you can get yourself a good education, get yourself a good job, you can raise yourself out of poverty … the arc that *The Fourth World War* takes is that it begins at this moment of capitalist decomposition where everyone's alone … it begins in the moment after war dissolves every form of human connection that you have and tries to bring the audience to a point at the end where … Marcos ends the film saying 'you will no longer be you, now you are us', you're part of a global movement of people and you're connected to human beings all over the planet in a way that is deeper than the connection that exists between a consumer and a producer, between an oppressor and the oppressed, or between … a victim and a criminal … when those kinds of connections of solidarity are successfully articulated … things can change.

Speaking a new language
of struggle and possibility

One of the most compelling dimensions of Zapatismo is the way in which it has introduced a new language of political struggle, identity and possibility. Instead of the bureaucratic language and rigid style used so often by other insurgent and revolutionary groups the political discourse of the Zapatistas is one alive with poetry, myth, wit and hope. This new political language — seen most clearly in Zapatista communiqués — communicates the promise of Zapatismo's provocations surrounding issues of vanguardism, the state, privileged identities of struggle, and innovative and inspiring tactics for social change. Equally importantly, this new language has in turn provoked the emergence of other discourses of political struggle and possibility elsewhere, new languages for new types of socio-political struggle and possibility transnationally. Of course, this does not mean that the Zapatistas themselves have worked out ideal solutions to the many and varied challenges of radical socio-political change. What it does mean is that through the process of working through difficult questions both internal and external to the movement — what the Zapatistas would call 'walking questioning' — Zapatismo has participated in provoking questions about not only the goal of social change but its very nature as well.

If the struggle for a new world is one to be undertaken by rebels engaged in diverse struggles in their particular contexts, Zapatismo has nevertheless served to catalyse the sense that this resistance and alternative-building is interconnected across time and space. In part, the ability of Zapatismo to function in such a way is illuminated by the manner in which the Zapatistas have situated themselves in relation to a multitude of other peoples in struggle. At the opening ceremonies of the First Intercontinental Encuentro for Humanity and Against Neoliberalism, the General Command of the EZLN explicitly articulated 'who we are' in a way that says much about how the Zapatistas view their struggle in relation to those of others:

> This is who we are.
> The Zapatista National Liberation Army.
> The voice that arms itself to be heard.
> The face that hides itself to be seen.
> The name that hides itself to be named.
> The red star who calls out to humanity and the world to be heard, to be seen, to be named.
> The tomorrow to be harvested in the past.

Behind our black mask,
Behind our armed voice,
Behind our unnameable name,
Behind us, who you see,
Behind us, we are you.
Behind we are the same simple and ordinary men and women,
    who are repeated in all races,
    painted in all colors,
    speak in all languages,
    and live in all places.
The same forgotten men and women.
The same excluded,
The same untolerated,
The same persecuted,
We are you.
Behind us, you are us.
Behind our masks is the face of all excluded women,
Of all the forgotten indigenous,
Of all the persecuted homosexuals,
Of all the despised youth,
Of all the beaten migrants,
Of all those imprisoned for their words and thoughts,
Of all the humiliated workers,
Of all those dead from neglect,
Of all the simple and ordinary men and women,
Who don't count,
Who aren't seen,
Who are nameless,
Who have no tomorrow.
(EZLN 2001b: 111–12)

The General Command's assertion of a shared identity with
a diversity of others facing oppression is a powerful rhetorical move because even as it affirms a common struggle it does
not erase or subsume difference. Combined with the evocative
poetic power characteristic of this and many other Zapatista
communiqués, Zapatismo's language and imagination of radical

socio-political change represent a fundamental departure from the bureaucratic and homogenizing discourse of so many other revolutionary movements.

The insistence on the irreducible diversity of struggles aimed at building a better world has been a hallmark of the Zapatistas' approach to political analysis and solidarity from the outset of their movement. The flexibility, humility and thoughtfulness with which the Zapatistas approach their own struggle for social justice have facilitated constructive dialogue with others in many different places. This unorthodox approach to radical socio-political change is woven through many Zapatista communiqués, but the joy and possibility of this position are nowhere better expressed than in a communiqué issued by Subcomandante Marcos in 1994 in reply to an allegation made in the Mexican press that he was a homosexual:

> Marcos is gay in San Francisco, a black person in South Africa, Asian in Europe, a Chicano in San Isidro, an anarchist in Spain, a Palestinian in Israel, an Indigenous person in the streets of San Cristóbal, a gang-member in Neza, a rocker on … campus, a Jew in Germany, an ombudsman in the Department of Defense …, a feminist in a political party, a communist in the post-Cold War period, a prisoner in Cintalapa, a pacifist in Bosnia, a Mapuche in the Andes, a teacher in National Confederation of Educational Workers, an artist without a gallery or a portfolio, a housewife in any neighborhood in any city in any part of Mexico on a Saturday night, a guerrilla in Mexico at the end of the twentieth century, a striker in the CTM, a sexist in the feminist movement, a woman alone in a Metro station at 10 p.m., a retired person standing around in the Zócalo, a campesino without land, an underground editor, an unemployed worker, a doctor with no office, a non-conformist student, a dissident against neoliberalism, a writer without books or readers, and a Zapatista in the Mexican Southeast. In other words, Marcos is a human being in this world. Marcos is every untolerated, oppressed, exploited minority that is resisting and saying, 'Enough!'

He is every minority who is now beginning to speak and every
majority that must shut up and listen. He is every untolerated group
searching for a way to speak, their way to speak. Everything that
makes power and the good consciences of those in power uncomfort-
able — this is Marcos. (1994)

Rather than fencing off and defending a strict political or
identity boundary, in both these quotations the Zapatistas reject
the notion that there is a single or even privileged position from
which to struggle and claim a 'true' revolutionary pedigree. As
rebels, they insist that the struggle 'for humanity and against
neoliberalism' — as well as against a variety of other oppressions
from racism to sexism to heterosexism — must be made up of
all the diversity that constitutes humanity. Facing allegations
of homosexuality, Marcos responds not by denying them and
reaffirming his heterosexual masculinity but by establishing the
identity of the rebel — represented here by the figure of Marcos
himself — as someone who embodies all those struggling against
oppression.

Three shoulders

In August 2004, Subcomandante Marcos issued a series of communiqués entitled 'Reading a Video' detailing the successes and
failures of the Zapatista struggle. In the third part of this series
entitled 'Three Shoulders', Marcos narrates a 'founding legend'
of the Zapatista communities: 'those who inhabit these lands
now have three shoulders. To the two shoulders that the usual
human beings have, the Zapatistas have added a third: that of the
national and international "civil societies"' (2004f). As Marcos
explains, this 'third shoulder' has been a vital element in the
Zapatista struggle, providing the Zapatista movement with invalu-
able support, and doing so not on the basis of charity but as an
expression of a shared commitment:

We believe that we have been fortunate. From its beginnings, our movement has had the support and kindness of hundreds of thousands of persons on the five continents. This kindness and this support have not been withdrawn, even in the face of personal limitations, of distances, of differences of culture and language, borders and passports, of differences in political concepts, of the obstacles put up by the federal and state governments, the military checkpoints, harassment and attacks, of the threats and attacks by paramilitary groups, of our mistrust, our lack of understanding of the other, of our clumsiness.

No, in spite of all of that (and of many other things which everyone knows) the 'civil societies' of Mexico and the world have worked because of, for and with us.

And they have done so not out of charity, nor out of pity, nor out of political fashion, nor out of a desire for publicity, but because they have, in one way or another, embraced a cause which is still, for us, great: the building of a world where all worlds fit, a world, that is, which carries the hearts of everyone. (2004f)

In the face of the failure of social democratic, Keynesian, and other technocratic approaches to ameliorating capitalism's worst consequences, the grotesque realities of 'revolutionary' socialist states such as the Soviet Union, and the arrogance of declarations of neoliberal capitalism and its trappings of liberal democracy as 'the end of history', Zapatismo offers visions of paths beyond these structural and ideological dead ends. Rather than forwarding a ten-point plan for revolutionary change for all people everywhere, Zapatismo on a transnational scale has instead offered radical, grassroots, hopeful and open-ended visions of socio-political change. Zapatismo's rebel appeal transnationally is in part attributable to the fact that it has provocatively sought to unsettle the perception that the familiar modern projects of both the left and the right are the only viable ones. But this rebel appeal is also due to the fact that Zapatismo transnationally is a provocation rather than a blueprint for radical socio-political change, a vision of possibility instead of revolutionary or reactionary science. The rebel quality of Zapatismo is central to its power and significance, particularly when it is juxtaposed to the poverty of mainstream political channels and discourse. Testing received boundaries, moving over rough and less travelled political terrain, offering an expansive vision of solidarity and social struggle, always challenging singular claims to power and truth, refusing to forsake the hope in radical social transformation leading to true social justice in exchange for a 'seat at the table' with powerholders — these are among the most important characteristics of Zapatismo's rebel appeal on a transnational scale.

'To open a crack in history'

CONCLUSION

ASKED WHAT THE Zapatistas wanted, Subcomandante Insurgente Marcos once replied, 'To open a crack in history' (2001e: 212). By this he meant that a core dimension to the Zapatista struggle was to reclaim dignity, hope and the possibility for a more just, free and democratic future. In essence, this statement — at once simple and tremendously complex — explains why the Zapatistas have exerted such influence as rebels nationally and transnationally. Instead of seeking to impose another blueprint for the revolutionary transformation of the nation, trying to seize power, or insisting that their path was *the path* to authentic social change, the Zapatistas have crafted a radical social change process that is collaborative, democratic, imaginative and unclosed. Not every initiative proposed by the Zapatistas has been successful, nor have the Zapatistas themselves escaped making errors, but their humility, honesty and deep desire to build a world marked by the mutual recognition of dignity — a 'world capable of holding many worlds' — has generated a rebel political philosophy and practice that have inspired others both near and far.

In this work, I have offered a critical overview of the significance of the Zapatistas as rebels on regional, national and transnational scales. For a movement whose base communities often lack basic necessities and have suffered — and resisted — through five centuries of creeping oblivion, the Zapatistas have managed to exert a moral, political and inspirational force far beyond their material capacities or concrete victories. Refusing to sell themselves or others out in order to win a 'seat at the table' with powerholders or to win narrow gains, the Zapatista rebels have reminded others globally that dignity, honesty and integrity are essential principles of any true revolutionary struggle. Beyond their prolific and poetic rhetoric, the Zapatistas have pursued a path of dialogue, encounter and engagement with a diversity of other rebels in struggle without compromising the core demands of their own struggle. Even as the Zapatistas sought to reach beyond the borders of Mexico to engage other rebels in an effort to crystallize an 'international order of hope' capable of contesting neoliberal capitalism, they were simultaneously working to build relations of good governance and autonomy in their own rebel territory. Rather than waiting for social justice, indigenous rights or a just and enduring peace to be bestowed upon them by political elites, the Zapatistas have repeatedly insisted — and demonstrated through their committed action — that these things are only achievable if people work together collectively to make them a reality.

At a moment when dreams of revolution seemed to have become utter anachronisms in the wake of the collapse of the Soviet Union and the global ascendancy of neoliberal capitalism and its trappings of liberal democracy, the Zapatista rebellion served as the bright spark of possibility and hope in an otherwise dark time. For others within and outside Mexico seeking some sort of confirmation that the future was still unwritten, the Zapatista rebels, by their very existence, confirmed it. Of course, this future is still very much up for grabs and, much as the Zapatista struggle itself, it is ultimately not so much a matter of 'winning' or 'losing' it but of making it as it unfolds.

There is no doubt that the Zapatistas no longer occupy headlines either nationally or internationally the way they once did. As this book has detailed, the constant work required to creatively engage 'civil societies' is considerable and, unfortunately, the Zapatistas have yet to find a mechanism or a form of organizing beyond their own communities that is capable of producing the widespread, radical and hopeful mass movement required to change things on national and transnational scales. This does not mean that the Zapatistas have failed, that their movement has withered, or that their time has passed. Indeed, at the time of writing, the Zapatistas have successfully built and defended the autonomy that has always been at the core of their rebellion. With five Zapatista Autonomous Rebel Municipal Zones operating in Chiapas, the Zapatistas have built the dignified, directly democratic, and autonomous socio-political and economic structures that powerholders so desperately sought to deny them. As evidenced by the recent Global Festival of Dignified Rage and the Other Campaign of which it is a part, the Zapatistas also continue to forge novel paths by which to engage other rebels regionally, nationally and transnationally in pursuit of a common struggle 'for humanity and against neoliberalism'.

At the same time, these initiatives have been hard pressed to match the power or success of earlier mobilizing efforts such as the March of the People of the Colour of Earth. In a media-saturated world where multiplying crises compete to claim the headline of the day or the week, the Zapatistas simply cannot provide the constant innovation and novelty necessary to maintain media focus. In addition to this, radical collective projects for social transformation on a global scale have faced considerable obstacles in recent years. While the summit-hopping spectacles of the alter-globalization movement were already on the wane in 2001, the 9/11 terrorist attacks provided the perfect rationale for even avowedly 'liberal democratic' states dramatically to ratchet up their security and surveillance powers, challenging the capacity for people to organize and mobilize as they had been. In Latin America, the rise to power of several left populist political leaders from Venezuela's Hugo Chávez to Bolivia's Evo Morales to Brazil's Luiz Inácio Lula da Silva — not to mention the meteoric rise to power of Barack Obama in the United States — has refocused the attention of many on the terrain of electoral politics as one of possibility and even hope.

Compounding all of this, a capitalist crisis of global proportions has driven many back into the territory of the familiar. In the Global North, the absence of radicalized mass movements demanding real change and a holding to account of the elites, institutions and system responsible for our current eco-social-economic crisis is striking. In their absence we see the revival of social-democratic policies, Keynesian economic theory, and a general hope that 'business as usual' will resume once this moment passes. The same fear of committing to a radical, serious project of socio-political and economic transformation which the Zapatistas constantly ran up against in their attempts to provoke 'civil society' to take some responsibility for saving itself is a global theme — but nowhere is it seen more blatantly than in the world's wealthiest enclaves as people turn in fear to those who promise to defend and revitalize the very capitalist system that got us here in the first place. These are challenging times indeed for movements seeking to build new worlds.

As for the Zapatistas, they never wanted to be the vanguard of a national, much less a global, movement, so perhaps it is fitting that they no longer function as a political and ethical lodestone for the largely defunct 'movement of movements'. This does not mean that the Zapatistas have been surpassed, are no longer relevant, or have no place in a renewed transnational struggle against neo-liberal capitalism and its capacity for generating ever-escalating social, ecological and economic crises. Rather, it points to the fact that on regional and transnational scales, we currently find ourselves in a moment where many movements, collectives and individual activists are reconsidering and reimagining new ways forward. The Zapatistas have been an essential element of this process since 1994, and when a renewed, innovative and powerful collective project for socio-political and economic transformation does emerge, its very existence will bear a great debt to the struggle of the Zapatistas.

In this work, I have sought to illuminate the key bases and effects of Zapatismo's rebel significance. From the deep roots of rebellion in Mexico to Zapatismo as political philosophy and practice, to the national and transnational influence of the Zapatista struggle, the Zapatistas appear not as 'professionals of violence', terrorists or criminals, but as *rebels* with all the legitimacy and symbolic power that label conveys. But the rebel influence of Zapatismo has not been — nor will it be — felt through the wearing of ski masks, the replication of their councils of good government, or the adoption of their rhetoric. Instead, Zapatismo's rebel significance has been felt through the creation of a new kind of politics rooted in the formation of new kinds of relationships and new kinds of spaces and practices which embody the principles of inclusivity, democracy, dignity and hope.

The rebel encounters with Zapatismo, whether they be physical encounters with the Zapatistas themselves or encounters mediated via Internet, email, DVDs, videos, text, or a host of other media, have provoked a wealth of responses. As really existing rebels and not merely symbols, the Zapatistas continue to deal with the dangers and difficulties of being a resistance movement deeply committed to the building of alternatives. Violence and persecution are daily consequences of occupying this position, and this is something those who have been inspired by the Zapatista rebels — particularly their international supporters — would do well to remember. Building a new world is hardly an easy task and it comes with consequences for those who choose to defy the dominant order and its machinery of coercion and repression. This is something that many rebels in the Global North need to recognize more completely and work diligently to build into their politics of solidarity.

Ultimately, it is vital to recall that the Zapatistas are not merely rebel icons, not simply symbols of resistance, but a living people in struggle. Their struggle does not exist simply to inspire rebels elsewhere and if it is to have enduring significance it will only be through the building of popular movements in the North as well as the South. These movements must be committed to building serious networks of communication and coordination among themselves in a struggle dedicated not to conquering the world but to making the world anew, to building a world in which many worlds fit.

References

Abdel-Moneim, Sarah Grussing (1996) 'Virtual Voices, Electronic Bodies: Women and Resistance in Cyber-Chiapas', paper delivered at Femunida Unidas Conference, 29 December. www.asu.edu/clas/dll/femunida/publications.htm.

Alfred, Taiaiake (2005) *Wasáse: Indigenous Pathways of Action and Freedom*. Peterborough: Broadview Press.

Alonso, Jorge (2009) 'Zapatistas Organize the First Global Festival of Dignified Rage', *Envio* 350. www.envio.org.ni/articulo/3940.

Appadurai, Arjun (1996) *Modernity at Large: Cultural Dimensions of Globalization*. Minneapolis: University of Minnesota Press.

Aridjis, Homero (2002) 'Indian is Beautiful', in Tom Hayden, ed., *The Zapatista Reader*. New York: Thunder's Mouth Press.

Ballesteros Corona, Carolina, and Patrick Cuninghame (1998) 'A Rainbow at Midnight: Zapatistas and Autonomy', *Capital & Class* 66: 12–22.

Bedregal, Ximena (1994) 'Chiapas: Considerations from Our Feminist Point of View', in Rosa Rojas, ed., *Chiapas y las mujeres que?* Mexico: Editiones La Correa Feminista, Centro de Investigacion y Capacitacion de la Mujer A.C. www.eco.utexas.edu/Homepages/Faculty/Cleaver/begin.html.

Bellinghausen, Hermann, and Gloria Muñoz Ramírez (2008) 'The Next Step: The Sixth Declaration of the Lacandón Jungle', in Gloria Muñoz Ramírez, *The Fire & the Word: A History of the Zapatista Movement*. San Francisco: City Lights Books.

Benjamin, Medea (1995) 'Interview: Subcomandante Marcos', in Elaine Katzenberger, ed., *First World, HA HA HA! The Zapatista Challenge*. San Francisco: City Lights Books.

Benjamin, Thomas (1996) *A Rich Land, a Poor People: Politics and Society in Modern Chiapas*. Albuquerque: University of New Mexico.

Big Noise Tactical (n.d.) 'About Us.' www.bignoisefilms.com/about.htm.

Cal y Mayor, Araceli Burguete (2003) 'The de Facto Autonomous Process: New Jurisdictions and Parallel Governments in Rebellion', in Jan Rus, Rosalva Aída Hernández Castillo and Shannan L. Mattiace, eds, *Mayan Lives, Mayan Utopias: The Indigenous Peoples of Chiapas and the Zapatista Rebellion*. Toronto: Rowman & Littlefield.

Callahan, Manuel (2004a) 'Zapatismo and Global Struggle: "A Revolution to Make a Revolution Possible"', in Eddie Yuen, Daniel Burton-Rose and George Katsiaficas, eds, *Confronting Capitalism: Dispatches from a Global Movement*. Brooklyn: Soft Skull Press.

—— (2004b) 'Zapatismo beyond Chiapas', in David Solnit, ed., *Globalize Liberation: How to Uproot the System and Build a Better World*. San Francisco: City Lights Books.

Carr, Barry (1992) *Marxism and Communism in Twentieth-Century Mexico*. Lincoln: University of Nebraska Press.

Clayton, Leah (1997) 'Revolutionary Zapatista Women in Cultural Perspective', *The Prism*. www.ibiblio.org/prism/Mar97/zapatista.html.

Cleaver, Harry (1998) 'The Zapatista Effect: The Internet and the Rise of an Alternative Political Fabric', *Journal of International Affairs* 51(2): 621–40.

Cockcroft, James (1998) *Mexico's Hope: An Encounter with Politics and History*. New York: Monthly Review Press.

Collier, George, and Elizabeth Quaratiello (1999) *Basta! Land and the Zapatista Rebellion in Chiapas*. Oakland CA: Food First Books.

de Marcellus, Olivier (2001) 'Peoples' Global Action: Dreaming Up an Old Ghost', in *Auroras of the Zapatistas: Local and Global Struggles of the Fourth World War*. Brooklyn NJ: Autonomedia.

Desai, Manisha (2002) 'Transnational Solidarity: Women's Agency, Structural Adjustment, and Globalization', in Nancy Naples and Manisha Desai, eds, *Women's Activism and Globalization: Linking Local Struggles and Transnational Politics*. New York: Routledge.

Eber, Christine (2003) 'Buscando una Nueva Vida: Liberation through

Autonomy in San Pedro Chenalhó, 1970–1998', in Jan Rus, Rosalva Aída Hernández Castillo and Shannan L. Mattiace, eds, *Mayan Lives, Mayan Utopias: The Indigenous Peoples of Chiapas and the Zapatista Rebellion*. Toronto: Rowman & Littlefield. Originally published in *Latin American Perspectives* 28(2): 45–72.

Enloe, Cynthia (1988) *Does Khaki Become You? The Militarization of Women's Lives*. Boston: Pandora.

Esteva, Gustavo (2003) 'The Meaning and Scope of the Struggle for Autonomy', in Jan Rus, Rosalva Aída Hernández Castillo and Shannan L. Mattiace, eds, *Mayan Lives, Mayan Utopias: The Indigenous Peoples of Chiapas and the Zapatista Rebellion*. Toronto: Rowman & Littlefield. Originally published in *Latin American Perspectives* 28(2): 120–48.

—— (1999) 'The Zapatistas and People's Power', *Capital & Class* 68: 153–82.

EZLN (Ejército Zapatista de Liberación Nacional) (2005) 'Sixth Declaration of the Lacandona, pt 3', trans. Irlandesa. chiapas95-english@eco.utexas.edu.

—— (2004a) Fifth Declaration of the Lacandón Jungle', in Žiga Vodovnik, ed., *¡Ya Basta! Ten Years of the Zapatista Uprising*. Oakland CA: AK Press. Communiqué originally issued 19 July 1998.

—— (2004b) 'Fourth Declaration of the Lacandón Jungle', in Žiga Vodovnik, ed., *¡Ya Basta! Ten Years of the Zapatista Uprising*. Oakland CA: AK Press. Communiqué originally issued 1 January 1996.

—— (2004c) 'Third Declaration of the Lacandón Jungle', in Žiga Vodovnik, ed., *¡Ya Basta! Ten Years of the Zapatista Uprising*. Oakland CA: AK Press. Communiqué originally issued 1 January 1995.

—— (2002) 'The People of the Color of the Earth', in Tom Hayden, ed., *The Zapatista Reader*. New York: Thunder's Mouth Press. Communiqué originally issued 11 March 2001.

—— (2001a) 'First Declaration of the Lacandón Jungle', in Subcomandante Insurgente Marcos, *Our Word is Our Weapon*, ed. Juana Ponce de León. Toronto: Seven Stories Press. Communiqué originally issued 2 January 1994.

—— (2001b) 'Opening Remarks at the First Intercontinental Encuentro for Humanity and Against Neoliberalism', in Subcomandante Insurgente Marcos, *Our Word is Our Weapon*, ed. Juana Ponce de León. Toronto:

Seven Stories Press. Remarks originally given on 27 July 1996 in Oventik, Chiapas.

—— (2001c) 'Second Declaration of La Realidad for Humanity and Against Neoliberalism', in Subcomandante Insurgente Marcos, *Our Word is Our Weapon*, ed. Juana Ponce de León. Toronto: Seven Stories Press. Communiqué originally issued August 1996.

—— (2001d) 'Second Declaration of the Lacandón Jungle', in Subcomandante Insurgente Marcos, *Our Word is Our Weapon*, ed. Juana Ponce de León. Toronto: Seven Stories Press. Communiqué originally issued 12 June 1994.

—— (1996) 'First Declaration of La Realidad for Humanity and Against Neoliberalism'. http://flag.blackened.net/revolt/mexico/ezln/ccri_1st_dec_real.html.

—— (1993) 'Women's Revolutionary Law'. http://flag.blackened.net/revolt/mexico/ezln/womlaw.html.

Flood, Andrew (2003) 'Dreaming of a Reality Where the Past and the Future Meet the Present', in Notes From Nowhere, ed., *We Are Everywhere: The Irresistible Rise of Global Anti-Capitalism*. London and New York: Verso.

Forces of National Liberation (2003) *Statutes of the Forces of National Liberation*. Montreal: Abraham Guillen Press and Arm the Spirit; statutes first published in Mexico on 6 August 1980.

Foweraker, Joe (1990) Popular Movements and Political Change in Mexico', in Ann Craig and Joe Foweraker, eds, *Popular Movements and Political Change in Mexico*. Boulder CO: Lynne Rienner.

García Márquez, Gabriel, and Roberto Pombo (2004) 'The Hourglass of the Zapatistas', in Tom Mertes, ed., *A Movement of Movements: Is Another World Really Possible?* London and New York: Verso. First published in English as 'The Punch-Card and the Hourglass', *New Left Review* 9 (May–June 2001): 69–79.

Gilbreth, Chris, and Gerardo Otero (2001) 'Democratization in Mexico: The Zapatista Uprising and Civil Society', *Latin American Perspectives* 28(4): 7–29.

Gillermoprieto, Alma (2002) 'The Unmasking', in Tom Hayden, ed., *The Zapatista Reader*. New York: Thunder's Mouth Press. Originally published in *The New Yorker,* 13 March 1995.

Gilly, Adolfo (2005) *The Mexican Revolution*. New York: New Press.

—— (1998) 'Chiapas and the Rebellion of the Enchanted World', in Daniel Nugent, ed., *Rural Revolt in Mexico: US Intervention and the Domain of Subaltern Politics*. Durham NC: Duke University Press.

Goetze, Diana (1997a) 'The Zapatista Women: The Movement from Within'. www.actlab.utexas.edu/~geneve/zapwomen/goetze/thesis.html.

—— (1997b) 'Revolutionary Women from Soldaderas to Comandante — The Roles of Women in the Mexican Revolution and the Current Zapatista Movement'. www.actlab.utexas.edu/~geneve/zapwomen/goetze/enterpaper.html.

Guevara, Ernesto Che (1961) *Guerrilla Warfare*. New York: Monthly Review Press.

Harvey, Neil (1998) *The Chiapas Rebellion: The Struggle for Land and Democracy*. Durham NC: Duke University Press.

Hellman, Judith A. (2000) 'Real and Virtual Chiapas: Magic Realism and the Left', in *Necessary and Unnecessary Utopias: Socialist Register 2000*, 161–186. London: Merlin Press.

Hernández Castillo, Rosalva Aída (1997) 'Between Hope and Adversity: The Struggle of Organized Women in Chiapas since the Zapatista Uprising', *Journal of Latin American Anthropology* 3(1): 102–20.

Hernández Navarro, Luis (2006) 'The Breaking Wave', in Subcomandante Marcos and the Zapatistas, *The Other Campaign*. San Francisco: City Lights Books.

—— (2002) Mexico's Secret War', in Tom Hayden, ed., *The Zapatista Reader*. New York: Thunder's Mouth Press. Originally published in *NACLA Report on the Americas* 32(1), May/June 1999.

—— (1994) 'The New Mayan War', *NACLA Report on the Americas* 27(5), March/April: 6–10.

Higgins, Nicholas (2000) 'The Zapatista Uprising and the Poetics of Cultural Resistance', *Alternatives* 25: 359–74.

Holloway, John (2002a) *Change the World without Taking Power: The Meaning of Revolution Today*. London: Pluto Press.

—— (2002b) 'Zapatismo and the Social Sciences', *Capital & Class* 78: 153–60.

Huizer, Gerrit (1970) 'Emiliano Zapata and the Peasant Guerrillas in the Mexican Revolution', in Rodolfo Stavenhagen, ed., *Agrarian Problems and Peasant Movements in Latin America*. Garden City NY: Doubleday.

Khasnabish, Alex (2008a) '"A Tear in the Fabric of the Present": The Rhizomatic Resonance of Zapatismo and Radical Activism in the North of the Americas', *Journal for the Study of Radicalism* 2(2): 27–52.

—— (2008b) *Zapatismo beyond Borders: New Imaginations of Political Possibility*. Toronto: University of Toronto Press.

—— (2007) 'Insurgent Imaginations', *Ephemera: Theory and Politics in Organization* 7(4): 505–26. www.ephemeraweb.org/journal/7-4/7-4 khasnabish.pdf.

Kimmel, Michael S. (2003) 'Globalization and Its Mal(e)contents: The Gendered Moral and Political Economy of Terrorism', *International Sociology* 18(3): 603–20.

Kingsnorth, Paul (2003) *One No, Many Yeses: A Journey to the Heart of the Global Resistance Movement*. London: Free Press.

Klein, Naomi (2002) 'Rebellion in Chiapas', in Debra Ann Levy, ed., *Fences and Windows: Dispatches from the Front Lines of the Globalization Debate*. Toronto: Vintage Canada. Originally published in *Guardian*, 3 March 2001.

Knudson, Jerry (1998) 'Rebellion in Chiapas: Insurrection by Internet and Public Relations', *Media, Culture & Society* 20: 507–18.

Leyva Solano, Xóchitl (1998) 'The New Zapatista Movement: Political Levels, Actors, and Political Discourse in Contemporary Mexico', in Valentina Napolitano and Xóchitl LeyvaSolano, eds, *Encuentros Antropologicos: Politics, Identity and Mobility in Mexican Society*. London: Institute of Latin American Studies.

Mattiace, Shannan (2003) 'Regional Renegotiations of Space: Tojolabal Ethnic Identity in Las Margaritas, Chiapas', in Jan Rus, Rosalva Aída Hernández Castillo and Shannan L. Mattiace, eds, *Mayan Lives, Mayan Utopias: The Indigenous Peoples of Chiapas and the Zapatista Rebellion*. Toronto: Rowman & Littlefield. Originally published in *Latin American Perspectives* 28(2): 73–97.

—— (1997) 'Zapata Vive! The EZLN, Indigenous Politics, and the Autonomy Movement in Mexico', *Journal of Latin American Anthropology* 3(1): 32–71.

Meyer, Jean (2002) 'Once Again, the Noble Savage', in Tom Hayden, ed., *The Zapatista Reader*. New York: Thunder's Mouth Press. Originally published in *Letras Libras*, 1998.

Monsiváis, Carlos (2002) 'From the Subsoil to the Mask that Reveals: The Visible Indian', in Tom Hayden, ed., *The Zapatista Reader*. New York: Thunder's Mouth Press. Originally published in *Proceso*, 3 March 2001.

Muñoz Ramírez, Gloria (2008) *The Fire and The Word: A History of the Zapatista Movement*. San Francisco: City Lights Books.

Navarro, Fernanda (1998) 'A New Way of Thinking Action: The Zapatistas in Mexico — A Postmodern Guerilla Movement?'. *Rethinking Marxism* 10(4): 155–65.

Notes From Nowhere, eds (2003) *We Are Everywhere: The Irresistible Rise of Global Anti-Capitalism*. London and New York: Verso.

Olesen, Thomas (2005) *International Zapatismo: The Construction of Solidarity in the Age of Globalization*. London: Zed Books.

Oppenheimer, Andres (2002) 'Guerrillas in the Mist', in Tom Hayden, ed., *The Zapatista Reader*. New York: Thunder's Mouth Press. Originally published in *The New Republic*, 1999.

Perez, Matilde, and Laura Castellanos (1994) 'Do Not Leave Us Alone! Interview with Comandanta Ramona', in Rosa Rojas, ed., *Chiapas y las mujeres que?* Mexico: Editiones La Correa Feminista, Centro de Investigacion y Capacitacion de la Mujer A.C. www.eco.utexas.edu/ Homepages/Faculty/Cleaver/begin.htm. Originally published in *Double Jornada*, 7 March 1994.

PGA (Peoples' Global Action) (n.d.) 'Brief History of PGA'. www.nadir. org/nadir/initiativ/agp/en/pgainfos/history.htm.

—— (n.d.) 'Hallmarks of Peoples' Global Action'. www.nadir.org/nadir/ initiativ/agp/free/pga/hallm.htm.

—— (n.d.) 'Peoples' Global Action Manifesto'. www.nadir.org/nadir/ initiativ/agp/en/pgainfos/.

—— (n.d.) 'Peoples' Global Action Organisational Principles'. www.nadir. org/nadir/initiativ/agp/cocha/principles.htm.

Poniatowska, Elena (2002) 'Women's Battle for Respect Inch by Inch', in Tom Hayden, ed., *The Zapatista Reader*. New York: Thunder's Mouth Press.

Ramonet, Ignacio (2002) 'Marcos Marches on Mexico City', in Tom Hayden, ed., *The Zapatista Reader*. New York: Thunder's Mouth Press. Originally published in *Le Monde Diplomatique*, April 2001.

Ross, John (2006) *¡Zapatistas!: Making Another World Possible — Chronicles of Resistance 2000–2006*. New York: Nation Books.

—— (2002) 'The Story of the Boot and the Chessboard', in Tom Hayden, ed., *The Zapatista Reader*. New York: Thunder's Mouth Press.

—— (2000) *The War Against Oblivion: The Zapatista Chronicles*. Monroe ME: Common Courage Press.

Rus, Jan, Rosalva Aída Hernández Castillo and Shannan L. Mattiace (2003) 'Introduction', in Jan Rus, Rosalva Aída Hernández Castillo and Shannan L. Mattiace, eds, *Mayan Lives, Mayan Utopias: The Indigenous Peoples of Chiapas and the Zapatista Rebellion*. Toronto: Rowman & Littlefield.

Russell, Adrienne (2005) 'Myth and the Zapatista Movement: Exploring a Network Identity', *New Media & Society* 7(4): 559–77.

Selbin, Eric (2003) 'Zapata's White Horse and Che's Beret: Theses on the Future of Revolution', in John Foran, ed., *The Future of Revolutions: Rethinking Radical Change in the Age of Globalization*. London: Zed Books.

Solnit, Rebecca (2004) *Hope in the Dark: Untold Histories, Wild Possibilities*. New York: Nation Books.

Stephen, Lynn (2002) *Zapata Lives! Histories and Cultural Politics in Southern Mexico*. Berkeley: University of California Press.

Subcomandante Marcos (2008) 'Audio Message', in Gloria Muñoz Ramírez, *The Fire and the Word: A History of the Zapatista Movement*. San Francisco: City Lights Books.

—— (2004a) 'A Death Has Been Decided', in Žiga Vodovnik, ed., *¡Ya Basta! Ten Years of the Zapatista Uprising*. Oakland CA: AK Press. Communiqué originally issued July 2003.

—— (2004b) 'FAQ on March', in Žiga Vodovnik, ed., *¡Ya Basta! Ten Years of the Zapatista Uprising*. Oakland CA: AK Press. Communiqué originally issued February 2001.

—— (2004c) 'The Death Train of the WTO', in Žiga Vodovnik, ed., *¡Ya Basta! Ten Years of the Zapatista Uprising*. Oakland CA: AK Press. Communiqué originally issued 12 September 2003.

—— (2004d) 'The Seven Loose Pieces of the Global Jigsaw Puzzle (Neoliberalism as a Puzzle)', in Žiga Vodovnik, ed., *¡Ya Basta! Ten Years of the Zapatista Uprising*. Oakland CA: AK Press. Communiqué originally issued June 1997.

—— (2004e) 'The Zapatistas Hike Up the Price of the Indigenous Mexican Blood', in Žiga Vodovnik, ed., *¡Ya Basta! Ten Years of the Zapatista Uprising*. Oakland CA: AK Press. Communiqué originally issued 9 February 1995.

—— (2004f) 'Three Shoulders'. http://flag.blackened.net/revolt/mexico/ezln2004/marcosshouldersAUG.html. Communiqué originally issued August 2004.

—— (2002a) 'Testimonies of the First Day', in Tom Hayden, ed., *The Zapatista Reader*. New York: Thunder's Mouth Press. Originally published in *La Jornada*, 19 January 1994.

—— (2002b) 'The Fourth World War Has Begun', in Tom Hayden, ed., *The Zapatista Reader*. New York: Thunder's Mouth Press. Communiqué originally appeared in *Le Monde Diplomatique*, September 1997.

—— (2001a) 'A Storm and a Prophecy — Chiapas: The Southeast in Two Winds', in *Our Word is Our Weapon*, ed. Juana Ponce de León. Toronto: Seven Stories Press. Communiqué originally issued 27 January 1994.

—— (2001b) *Our Word is Our Weapon*, ed. Juana Ponce de León. Toronto: Seven Stories Press.

—— (2001c) 'The Retreat is Making Us Almost Scratch the Sky', in *Our Word is Our Weapon*, ed. Juana Ponce de León. Toronto: Seven Stories Press. Communiqué originally issued 20 February 1995.

—— (2001d) 'The Word and the Silence', in *Our Word is Our Weapon*, ed. Juana Ponce de León. Toronto: Seven Stories Press. Communiqué originally issued 12 October 1995.

—— (2001e) 'To Open a Crack in History', in *Our Word is Our Weapon*, ed. Juana Ponce de León. Toronto: Seven Stories Press. Communiqué originally issued September 1999.

—— (1994) 'Communiqué About the End of the Consultations', in *Zapatistas! Documents of the New Mexican Revolution*. Brooklyn NJ: Autonomedia. http://lanic.utexas.edu/project/Zapatistas/chapter11.html.

Tarrow, Sidney (2005) *The New Transnational Activism*. Cambridge: Cambridge University Press.

Vodovnik, Žiga (2004) 'The Struggle Continues…', in Žiga Vodovnik, ed., *¡Ya Basta! Ten Years of the Zapatista Uprising*. Oakland CA: AK Press.

Warman, Arturo (1976) *'We Come to Object': The Peasants of Morelos and the National State*. Baltimore MD: Johns Hopkins University Press.

Weinberg, Bill (2000) *Homage to Chiapas: The New Indigenous Struggles in Mexico*. London and New York: Verso.

Wolf, Eric (1969) *Peasant Wars of the Twentieth Century*. New York: Harper.

Womack, Jr, John (1999) *Rebellion in Chiapas*. New York: New Press.

—— (1968) *Zapata and the Mexican Revolution*. New York: Vintage.

Wood, Lesley J. (2004) 'Bridging the Chasms: The Case of Peoples' Global Action', in Joe Bandy and Jackie Smith, eds, *Coalitions across Borders: Transnational Protest and the Neoliberal Order*. Lanham MD: Rowman & Littlefield.

Index

Insurgent Lieutenant Colonel Moisés, 162
Intercontinental Encuentro for Humanity and Against Neoliberalism, 130, 136, 139; proposed location, 140
Internet warriors, Zapatistas as jibe, 165–6
Isadora, EZLN combatant, 75
Israel, Defence Force, 161

Jeffries, Fiona, 179
Juárez, Benito, 27, 29
Juntas de Buen Gobierno (JBG), 155–6
justice, Zapatista notion of, 90–92

Keynesianism, revival of, 197, 202
King Jr, Martin Luther, 174–5
Kingsnorth, Paul, 172, 179
Klein, Naomi, 174

La Garrucha, Chiapas community, 178
Las Margaritas, Chiapas, 67
la montaña, 70
La Realidad Chiapas village community, 140, 148, 178
Labastida, Francisco, 148
Lacandón Jungle, 56, 59, 70; Declarations of, *see above*; new migrant communities, 68
land: Brazil occupations, 182; collective ownership, 153; concentrated ownership, 48; *ejidos, see above*; government monopolized distribution, 43, 47; occupation, 67; ownership 'liberalisation', 27–8; redistribution, 35; 'reform', 24, 47
language(s): Mayan dialects, 13; new political, 171–2, 192–3; Spanish learning, 75, 79
Las Abejas (Bees), 145
Le Monde Diplomatique, 150
Lecumberri Prison, 37
Leyva Solano, Xóchitl, 100
'liberalisation', land ownership, 27–8
Liberating Army of the South, 31, 33,

36, 38
liberation theology, 49
liberty, Zapatista notion of, 89
López Obrador, Andrés Manuel, 160
Los Altos, Chiapas, 130, migration from, 68
'low intensity warfare', 8; US desired, 142
Lula da Silva, Luiz Inácio, 202

Madero, Francisco, 31, 34–5; coup against, 36, 38; murder of, 37
Major Susana, 77
Malcolm X, 175
Mandela, Nelson, 118
Maoism, 49
March for Indigenous Dignity, 149
March of the People of the Colour of Earth, 149, 154, 201
MAREZs, resource distribution, 156
Marxism: dogmatic, 'defeat' of, 56, 69; structural, 15
masks, Zapatista use, 12–13, 203
mass movements 1970s, 50
Maximilian, Archduke, 27
Mayans: Chiapas, 2, 55, 66–70; culture lifeworlds, 106; Yucatan conscripted, 23
Mayor Moisés, 7, 148
Mazariegos, Diego de, statue toppling, 60
Medellín conference 1968, 49
Menchú, Rigoberta, 118
Mexican Communist Party, 49
Mexican Constitution, 43, 112; Article 27, 44, 59; Article 39, 103, 110
Mexican Revolution 1910, 29, 41, 67; legacy use, 52, 54, 57; mythology of, 47; US hostility, 36; Zapatista struggle, 34
Mexico, 52; Association of Civil Organizations for Peace (CONPAZ), 10; embassy protests, 169; financial crisis 1976–77, 52; French military intervention, 27, 29; independence struggles, 25; independent indigenous

movement, 103; nation-building, 22; National Human Rights Commission, 9, 11; 1995 financial bailout, 14, 122; population conservatism, 143; presidential elections, *see below*; racist history, 149; 'rebel', 100, 106

Mexico City, 1; 'bureaucratic pivot', 25; National Anthropology School, Mexico City, 151; National Autonomous University of Mexico, 15, 152; peasant armies occupation, 40; pro-Zapatista demonstrations, 16; Tlatelolco massacre, 51; Zapatista 'taking', 151

militant leftism, 1960s, 49
militarization, women, 76
military bases, Chiapas, 148
military checkpoints, state use of, 8
Mitterrand, Danielle, 138
Moctezuma, Esteban, 121
modernity, as non-excluding, 105
modernization, dictatorial 'liberal', 29
Mondragón, General, 37
Monsiváis, Carlos, 118
Montes Azules, UNESCO biosphere, 126
Morales, Evo, 202
Morelia, Chiapas community, 178
Morelos, José María, 25–6, 47; agrarian revolution, 41
Mothers of the Plaza de Mayo, Argentina, 139
MST (Landlesss Workers' Movement), Brazil, 182
Mulroney, Brian, 168
Muñoz Ramírez, Gloria, 144

NAFTA (North American Free Trade Agreement), 1, 5, 100, 104, 168; fast-tracked, 62; implementation, 58; renegotiation demand, 140
narratives of struggle, diffusion, 167
nation-state: building, 21, 43; dominant ideology of, 86; national identity, 104
National Action Party (PAN), Mexico,

88, 148; media allies, 160
National and International Consultation for Peace, 128–9, 131
National Anthropology School, Mexico City, 151
National Autonomous University of Mexico, 15, 152
National Commission of Intermediation, Chiapas (CONAI), 10, 127–8, 144
National Consultation, on the Constitution, 147
National Democratic Convention, Aguascalientes 1994 (CND), 117–20, 124–5, 128; failure of, 130
National Indigenous Congress, 103, 136, 141
National Indigenous Institute, 49, 66
National Liberation Movement (MLN), 50, 120, 123–5; failure of, 130
national sovereignty, defence of, 158
National Strike council, non-sectarian, 51
nationalization, key resources, 46
Navarro, Fernanda, 93
neoliberalism: global restructuring, 79; policies, 52–3; trade agreements, 168
networks of resistance, intercontinental, 180, 186
new subjectivities, formation of, 187
New York City, Big Noise Tactical, 186
9/11 attacks, impact of, 3, 202
'No', politics of, 92–4
Norte, Chiapas, 130
Northern Division, 38–9
Notes from Nowhere, 173

Obama, Barack, 202
Obregón, Alvaro, 37–9, 41
Ocosingo, 67; battle in, 6
Olmos, Edward James, 138
Organization of American States (OAS), 145
'Other Campaign', 159–62, 201
Oventik, Chiapas community, 178

'walking questioning', 84, 193
'War on Terror': criminality labelling,
  3; unlimited, 170
Warman, Arturo, 40
Wars of Independence, Mexico, 25
Wilson, Henry Lane, 37
Womack Jr, John, 9, 11, 124, 127
women: childbirth deaths, 79; EZLN
  visibility, 76–7; indigenous,
  78; indigenous 'essentialism'
  questioning, 80; Spanish language
  literacy, 75
Women's Revolutionary Law, 76–8,
  80–81
World Bank, 181; 'Plan Chiapas', 57
WTO (World Trade Organization),
  181; Seattle protest, 167

Yucatan, independence declaration,
  23

Zapata, Emiliano, 31–40, 46–7, 70, 110,
  175; assassination of, 42–3; iconic
  figure, 71; legacy reclaimed, 102;
  state power rejection, 41
Zapatismo: as 'intuition', 83;
  communicative action, 85;
  discourse of, 84; radically
  democratic nature, 71
Zapatista Autonomous Rebel
  Municipal Zones, 155, 201
Zapatista command, arrest warrants
  for, 125–6
Zapatista Front of National Liberation,
  proposed, 134–5

Zapatistas: agriculture disruption, 139;
  'Aguascalientes' building, 127–30;
  anti-globalization movement, 167;
  armed insurgency rejection, 100;
  as catalysts, 116, 136, 184, 193; base
  communities, 74, 136, 166; caravan
  2001, 149, 151, 153; 'civil society'
  support call, 132; communicating
  style, 104, 107; communiqué style,
  194–6; community assemblies,
  108; dialogue, 177; discourse, 87,
  90–2; EZLN, see above; FZLN,
  see above; inclusive project, 113;
  indigenous history emphasis, 131;
  influence of, 3, 199; innovative
  political projects, 104; international
  response to, 138, 165, 169, 178;
  living people in struggle, 204;
  Mexican character emphasis, 86;
  negative impacts of, 106; new
  political language, 171–2, 192,
  200; non-terrorist perception of,
  105; original, 35–6, 42; 'Other
  Campaign', 159–62, 201; outside
  attention decrease, 201; rebel
  praxis, 82, 106, 177; self-criticism
  ability, 162; solidarity activism,
  189; struggle specificity assertion,
  94; transnational influence, 64, 97,
  185–7, 203; women's full rights,
  175; Zedillo offensive against, 15
Zedillo, Ernesto, 14–17, 119–22, 125–7,
  136–8, 141, 145
Zócalo Square demonstration, 12
  January 1994, 10